3D OF HAPPINESS

3D OF
HAPPINESS

Pleasure, Meaning
& Spirituality

Based on Science, Philosophy
& Personal Experience

Necati Aydin, Ph.D.

NEW YORK

LONDON • NASHVILLE • MELBOURNE • VANCOUVER

3D OF HAPPINESS
Pleasure, Meaning & Spirituality
Based on Science, Philosophy & Personal Experience

Published in New York, New York, by Morgan James Publishing. Morgan James is a trademark of Morgan James, LLC. www.MorganJamesPublishing.com

ISBN 978-1-64279-697-1 paperback
ISBN 978-1-64279-698-8 eBook
Library of Congress Control Number: 2019908635

Cover Design by:
Jonathan Lewis
Jonathan@jonlincreative.com

Morgan James is a proud partner of Habitat for Humanity Peninsula and Greater Williamsburg. Partners in building since 2006.

Get involved today! Visit
www.MorganJamesBuilds.com

Table of Contents

Preface

For many people, life is nothing but a search for happiness. Perhaps, the entire history of humanity is a search for happiness. Ironically, the search is not yet over. This book covers my happiness journey along with those of great thinkers such as Aristotle, Nietzsche, and Tolstoy. **My journey began with having almost nothing. I was at the bottom one percentile, worse than 99% of all people in the world. Over two decades, I managed to move to the top one percentile. I became better than 99% of people in terms of money and prestige. I ended with finding everything I wanted except happiness.**

Through my personal and academic journey, I came to the realization that we fail to find happiness because we search for it in the wrong place (dimension). Free market capitalism urges us to achieve happiness through the pursuit of more possessions, more experience, and a higher position. We work day and night to reach happiness. With each success of having, doing, being, and loving, we think we are almost there. Then, we soon realize we are not. When we fail, the capitalist compass will point to another target for us to reach happiness. Every time we set a goal to achieve happiness, we end up finding we need to do even more. This is what we call the "DEAD loop" which consists of **D**eprivation, **E**mulation, **A**chievement, and **D**isappointment. We argue that most happiness journeys with having, doing, being, and loving end up with the DEAD loop. **It begins with deprivation of the perceived means of happiness and emulation of those who**

have it. It ends with the accomplishment of having those means, but the disappointment of not having happiness.

The journey of searching for happiness reminds me of an interesting story of farmers. They came up with an intelligent way to make their donkeys go fast when traveling to their farms. They would attach a half-meter stick to the nose of their donkey. They would tie some delicious hay on the far edge of the stick. The donkey would think that he is only a half meter away from happiness (eating the hay). He would run to the hay. Since he was almost there, he would keep running faster and faster. However, it was not he, but the farmer who would reach his goal with every additional step. Likewise, we consider capitalists to be like the farmers in the story treating the consumer like the donkey. The hay is the promised happiness through having, doing, being, and loving. It does not matter how fast we are in getting there; it is clear that those objects are sheer deception that serve capitalists to maximize profit, rather than bring happiness.

The book consists of four parts. **The first part covers my happiness journey with having, doing, being, and loving through the pleasure (hedonic) dimension.** By having, we mean possessing something to be happy about, such as having nice clothes, a fancy house, a great car, etc. It is all about possessing something material as a means to be happy or happier. By doing, we mean experiencing, such as traveling, watching, playing. Doing is all about entertainment and fun activities. Despite some overlap with having and doing, we think it is essential to consider them as separate elements of the human journey. The former focuses on possession, while the latter refers mainly to sheer experience. By being, we mean position or status such as being a respected teacher, engineer, scientist, etc. It is all about gaining a certain status or respect in the eyes of others. It might be through a career or other activities. By loving, we mean relationship with others. We consider both friendship and romantic love. My journey for hedonic happiness will end with the confession that I was very successful with having, doing, being, and loving, but still failed to find happiness. This is what I call the "DEAD loop" of the hedonic dimension. The first part will end with the discussion of scientific research on that dimension.

The second part covers the earthly meaning (eudemonic) dimension of happiness. It begins with the search for eudemonic happiness by Aristotle.

Then, it continues with my journey for eudemonic happiness through meaning and believing. It ends with the scientific research of eudemonic happiness.

The third part includes the confession of not finding happiness through either pleasure or meaning dimension. It covers the failed paradise promised by free-market capitalism. It presents data on how "American dream" turns to nightmare for many people. It ends with Nietzsche's nihilism, which defines the ultimate outcome of life as the infinite nothing.

The fourth part covers the spiritual (G-donic) dimension of happiness. It begins with the very definition of the spiritual dimension I developed along with its underlying principles. Then, it covers my own journey of searching for happiness in the spritual dimension. It also discusses Tolstoy's journey of finding happiness through faith. It ends with scientific findings of that dimension.

If you want to know where you stand in your search for happiness, you can measure three dimensions of your happiness through the questionnaire provided at the very end.

In short, I began my happiness journey hoping to be happy through having, doing, and being what I like. My failure to find happiness through them led me to discover other dimensions of happiness. As science reveals through the discovery of DNA helix that life is built on a three-dimensional structure, scientific studies and ancient wisdom indicate that true happiness is also built on three dimensions. Indeed, **we argue that life is three dimensional both at biological and psychological levels.** We invite you to read this book to see how you could enrich your life experience by building your own 3D of happiness.

Acknowledgments

I shall begin with a sincere appreciation to mom and dad who raised me in a village with very limited resources. Special thanks go to my uncle and aunt who hosted me for three years in a small three-bedroom house despite having ten children of their own. Perhaps, if it were not for their very kind support, I would still be a shepherd in the village. I shared the draft manuscript with many individuals. I particularly appreciate very helpful feedback from Dr.Muhammed Bozdag and Dr.Mahshid Turner, Sarah Aljuraywi, Yousef Aseafan, Sabreen Abdulrahman, Sultan Alshathri, and Sadeem Alsofyani. I am really in debt to my professional editor, Katharine Worthington for her great editing and helpful input. Finally, many thanks to Morgan James Publishing team and its CEO, David Hancock, for their excellent guidance and great support during the publication process. While I acknowledge with gratitude my debt to these colleagues, I must emphasize that I, alone, am responsible for any mistakes and shortcomings in this book. And above all, for her sacrifices and shared responsibilities for 25 years, special thanks to my wife, Aynur, and our six children: Nurefsan, Berfinnur, Aishanur, Fatma Zehra, Kubranur, and Ibrahim Said.

Introduction

Defining Happiness with Three Dimensions

What would you prefer to be in life: a happy animal or an unhappy human? In other words, would you choose happiness or humanity? Assume that if you choose the former, you could be any animal you want. You would have the best of everything as an animal and live a happy life. However, if you choose the latter, you would be a miserable person experiencing nothing but hardship, difficulties, calamities, illness, oppression, etc.[1] If you do not like either option, then imagine an 'experience machine' developed by scientists. Assume that you can program into the machine whatever experiences you want to have. Once you hook yourself up to this machine, your experiences would be indistinguishable from real life experience. You could choose to live out your entire life in the machine, experiencing whatever pleasures and feelings you desire as if they were really happening. Assume that the machine works without any flaws. Now, would you be willing to hook up to such a machine for the rest of your life?

---

1   Two centuries ago when utilitarianism emerged, philosopher John S. Mill famously objected to the movement by stating, "It is better to be a human being dissatisfied than a pig satisfied; better to be Socrates dissatisfied than a fool satisfied." In modern times, I asked the above question of people in several different countries while giving a talk. I found out the majority of people would prefer to be a happy animal over an unhappy human.

The response to the questions above reveals your philosophy of happiness. It shows whether you think happiness is money and pleasure or meaning and accomplishment. In everyday life, people associate happiness with many different things. Like many, we believe that we are happy: "if we get what we want", "if we enjoy our life", "if everything in our life goes well", "if we are content with our life", "if we are having a problem-free life", "if we are at peace with ourselves", "if we have net positive pleasure when we compare our pain and pleasure", "if we have fun", "if we are lucky" and so on. Even though all of those statements are related to happiness, none of them provide an unequivocal definition of happiness.

In this book, happiness is defined as life satisfaction once we evaluate everything in life. Thus, a sick person could still be happy despite experiencing pain. A poor person might still be happy if he/she has something that provides satisfaction beyond what money could buy. On the other hand, a wealthy person might enjoy many material pleasures, but still, be unhappy when considering the entire life experience. Thus, happiness is defined as overall life satisfaction when we take everything into consideration. It is not about the state of our emotions based on present experience. It is about the state of our mind while reflecting on our entire life experience, which includes past, present, and future.

We argue that the failure to find happiness is due to our narrow understanding of happiness. It is crucial to recognize the multi-dimensional nature of happiness. Thus, we have redefined happiness within three models based on the corresponding dimensions: Hedonic (pleasure seeking), Eudemonic (earthly meaning), and G-donic (transcendental and spiritual meaning).

Flatland (Abbott 1963), a book published two centuries ago, serves as a great example to understand the differences between these three happiness models with three dimensions. A dot has no dimension; thus, it is a zero-dimensional object. A line has one dimension, which is the length. A polynomial shape such as square, triangle, the rectangle has two dimensions, which are length and width. Sphere, cone, cube are examples for three-dimensional shapes with length, width, and height. *Flatland* is an attempt to explain the difference between two and three-dimensional worlds. Some characters in the book are born in the two-dimensional world. For them, there is only height and length. There is no depth.

There is just left and right at the same level. Everything is flat. There is no up and down. When one character in the two-dimensional world encountered another in a three-dimensional world, he was puzzled to learn that you could look from above and see what was going to happen. The book provides an excellent account of the perceptional difference between those who live in a two- versus the three-dimensional world.

A geometrical dimension can be used as an analogy for the happiness dimensions in our models. The hedonic happiness model has one dimension, which is utility or pleasure maximization. The ultimate goal is to achieve the maximum possible pleasure. Like a line, its length could be long or short. It could be curved or straight. It does not matter; it moves along with no understanding of right, left, above, and below. If we lived in a one-dimensional world, we would only see eye to eye, but not the entire body. We would have no sense of reality beyond what appears to our eyes as a one-dimensional object. Similarly, for the hedonist, nothing exists but the purpose of pleasure and pain. The objective is to avoid pain and pursue pleasure.

Examples of One-Dimensional Shapes

Eudemonic happiness adds a second dimension, meaning, to the utility. Rather than living life just to create a line that is doomed to disappear, we try to close the line and make some meaningful shape as shown below:

Examples of Two-Dimensional Shapes

In the two-dimensional world, we can have a sense of right and left in addition to backward and forward. We can assign meaning to our shapes. However, we still have no sense of above and below. Thus, we will be on flat land in which we can only see one face of reality. If something is hidden below or above something else, it will be a mystery for us. We cannot know what is hidden. Thus, we will establish a life based on what is evident to us without knowing the ultimate reality. We will be no different from those prisoners in a cave who know nothing but shadows. Indeed, the shadow is a two-dimensional reality. It does not matter how much meaning we assign to the shapes; in the end, we will have nothing but disappointment.

In the three-dimensional world, we produce the G-donic dimension by adding spirituality to pleasure and meaning. We realize that the shadowy reality in the universe is just a manifestation of the transcendental reality beyond this life. Therefore, our objective is neither to have a longer line (hedonic) nor a meaningful shape (eudemonic); we want to have eternity, which transcends this transient life. Though many scholarly works discuss the first and second dimensions of happiness, we are the first to conceptualize and empirically analyze the third dimension.

Examples of Three-Dimensional Shapes

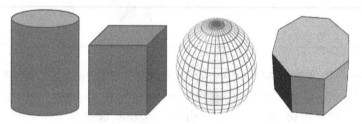

Higher Happiness in Higher Dimensions

In *3D of Happiness*, we do not suggest a form of ascetic life in terms of abstaining from worldly pleasure. Instead, we present a way of achieving higher happiness through exploring highest pleasure, meaning, and spirituality by having, doing, being, and loving. As shown below, we can imagine three dimensions of happiness through XYZ coordinates. X-axis shows pleasure, Y-axis meaning, and Z-axis spirituality. Pursuing happiness through pleasure alone means to be on the X-axis, moving along the one-dimensional line. Adding meaning to our happiness journey takes us to a two-dimensional flat area. Adding spirituality brings depth into our journey by taking us to a three-dimensional area. Of course, in each dimension, we have a long range of variation. Using the scale of zero to ten, we can achieve the highest happiness at point P, as shown in the chart below:

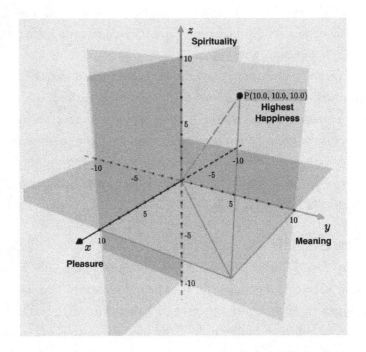

We argue that the hedonic dimension is limited to pursuing pleasure while the eudemonic and G-donic dimensions go beyond pleasure. Thus, moving to a higher dimension does not negate the outcome in the lower dimensions. Instead, it enriches life experience by driving a higher outcome. Indeed, one could drive different outcomes from the same experience depending on the dimensions.

For instance, in the hedonic dimension, the purpose is to be happy through maximizing sensual pleasure from eating. Thus, eating is not just fuel for the body; it is an essential means of pleasure. We will seek the best restaurants and try the best meals to experience the higher pleasure of eating. We will feel unhappy if we do not have the opportunity to eat enjoyable food.

In the eudemonic dimension, our primary goal is not pleasure maximization, but meaning maximization. We value food as fuel to help us to achieve something meaningful in life. Therefore, we do not necessarily look for the best food to be happy in life. Of course, we could still eat good food and experience great sensual pleasure. However, even if we eat at the best restaurant in the world, we could not be satisfied if we do not have a meaningful outcome in our daily life. On the other hand, we can still be happy if we manage to produce a meaningful outcome but fail to enjoy great food.

In the G-donic dimension, similar to the eudemonic dimension, our aim is not to maximize pleasure through eating the best food. Instead, our objective is to realize the transcendental reality. Thus, food is not just fuel for the body; it is also food for the mind, in terms of being a meaningful sign of transcendental reality. It is like a coded message. As we eat food, we will try to read its coded message about the transcendental reality. We will seek true satisfaction in finding the transcendental meaning of life.

Three Stages of Life

We can also liken three-dimensional happiness models to the three stages of life described by Kierkegaard to define the human journey. At the first stage, esthetic life, the purpose is to seek pleasure through various forms. The esthetic person does not reflect on the meaning of life. The pleasure-seeking self is dominant. There is no regard for moral laws set by society. However, if a person lives long enough, he will eventually experience despair. Then, he will move to the second stage, the ethical one. The moral person recognizes good and evil and respects social norms. She will try to be happy by living in conformity with social values. However, this stage is not sufficient to avoid despair altogether. The individual will not be satisfied with moral life. He needs to move to religious life by pursuing eternity. The religious stage is the recognition of a transcendental dimension beyond the phenomenal reality.

Three life stages work well with our three-dimensional happiness models. In the first stage, the esthetic person pursues hedonic happiness. Even though in the beginning, the hedonist seems to gain great pleasure, she would eventually experience despair. In the second stage, the ethical person pursues eudemonic happiness by engaging in socially and culturally meaningful acts. However, this happiness is not lasting, either. The moral person would eventually hit despair because she could not be satisfied with temporal meaning. In the third stage, the spiritual person would seek G-donic happiness by seeking satisfaction through transcendental reality.

Fulfilled Life and Happiness

In this book, we would like you to examine your life by asking big questions. We want you to reflect on the fruit of your works. That is because authentic happiness is possible only through a fulfilled life and unleashed potential. In his masterpiece *Mathnavi Ma'navi* ("Spiritual Couplet"), the 13th-century poet Rumi compares the human to a goose's egg placed under a hen for incubation along with many hen's eggs. Even though the chick from the goose's egg will become a goose, if she imitates her siblings, she can only walk. However, if she becomes aware of her potential, she can walk on the ground, swim in the water, and fly in the air.

Similarly, if we truly become aware of the critical elements of our nature, we can use them to move to higher dimensions and enjoy higher happiness. We shall realize that we do not consist of the body alone. We have a mind and soul as well. Therefore, we cannot be satisfied with bodily pleasure alone. We shall not limit our pursuit of happiness to sensual pleasure. We shall also seek higher intellectual and spiritual pleasures, which are the byproduct of unleashing our potential to have a transcendental experience through knowing, meaning, and spirituality.

PART I
SEEKING HAPPINESS IN PLEASURE (HEDONIC) DIMENSION

Chapter 1

Born in A Deprived Village

"Life itself is neither a good nor an evil: life is where good, or evil find a place, depending on how you make it for them."
—Michel de Montaigne

I was born in a village far east of Turkey. Even though the time of my birth was in the 20th Century, the society in which I was born was more typical of the Middle Ages. It was a primitive agricultural society that lacked many things we consider to be necessities in modern life. An overview of living conditions in the village will help you understand my background before I describe my lifelong journey of searching for happiness.

No Modern Housing and Heating

The village had no modern housing. Except for those built by the government, the houses were mostly made out of stone and mud. There was no use of cement. The houses were quite primitive, small, and simple. Having furniture or factory-made carpet was a sign of wealth. It was a dream for women to have anything beyond essential utensils. Even having a fork was considered to be luxury. Families would take extreme care to protect limited modern kitchen items.

Ironically, hand-made rugs were common, but not considered valuable. Instead, the villagers would dream of having a factory-made carpet.

The extended family generally lived under the same roof. One room was for the grandma and grandpa. One room was for the mom, dad, and kids. Usually, one room would be left for guests if the family was wealthy. The house would have sleeping and sitting rooms, but no kitchen, no toilet, and no bath or shower. A separate unit adjacent to the animal barn would be used for these functions. Cooking was done by burning wood or animal waste in that unit. The villagers would dry animal waste to use for heating and cooking. They also would cut trees from the nearby forest to prepare for the long and cold winter. Having the stove on all the time was a luxury. Since the temperature was mostly below zero for almost six months of the year, finding a warm house was a source of great pleasure for the villagers. The villagers would wear enough clothing to keep warm rather than burn limited wood and animal waste.

In the summertime, the villagers would move to a high plateau for their livestock. The life condition there was extremely harsh compared to the village, particularly during rainy weather. We would live in a simple tent on the plateau for 2-3 months. It was rare to find a tent that did not leak when raining. The tent would pose a security problem as well. Though the villagers would trust each other, it was vulnerable to uninvited guests from the animal kingdom, particularly at night. Thus, the challenge for the villagers was even higher during the summer time.

No Running Water

There was no running water. A fountain in the middle of the village provided water for drinking, cleaning, and showers. The villagers would carry water from the basin to their houses every day. They had to be very careful not to waste water, even when taking a shower. For those who lived in the outskirts of the village, it was not an easy job to carry water by hand, but the villagers had no option. Indeed, they were happy that they had the fountain. In the old days, they had to carry water from a nearby river to the village. Carrying water was an essential daily routine for the villagers, considered by the culture to be a female job. It was sporadic for a male to do this work.

The fountain provided an interesting public domain for the villagers. It was an excellent platform for females to share the news. Indeed, most enjoyed going to the fountain to chat with others. Since there was no phone, no TV or radio, and no coffee shop, the fountain was the only public domain for females to socialize.

The adaptation principle was working well for the villagers. They could adapt to life without running water. Even though in modern times, we can hardly imagine a happy life without running water, the villagers were quite happy for good reasons. First of all, there was no house in the village that had running water. Thus, there was no reason to compare and complain. Second, many studies indicate that humans quickly adapt to both good and adverse living conditions. Thus, the villagers would become accustomed to their daily suffering and consider it to be normal. Likewise, those in a town with running water would get used to the standard of having running water and take it for granted. Eventually, they both are at the same level of life satisfaction.

No Variety of Food and Clothing

There was no shortage of basic food. No one was starving. Indeed, the villagers would make sure that everyone had the minimum necessities. However, the variety of food was minimal. The essential diet would include bread and dairy products along with a few other items such as eggs, potatoes, onions, rice, lentil, and macaroni. Even though the villagers raised farm animals, they rarely had fresh meat. Indeed, they would slaughter an animal only if they had a special guest or an event such as a wedding. It was rare to find a house with a regular daily hot meal. Even sugar and tea were in limited supply. Having dessert was extremely rare. It was a tradition to make a simple dessert (halwa) when a new baby was born. The villagers were familiar with only several kinds of fruit such as apple, orange, pear, watermelon, melon, and grape. Most villagers would have a small garden to grow vegetables such as tomatoes, cucumber, green beans, etc.

There was no variety in clothing. The villagers would knit warm clothes such as a sweater for the long winter. They would wear their two or three sets of clothes until they were completely worn out. Indeed, it was prevalent to wear clothes with patches. Having several kinds of fabrics was a sign of wealth.

Villagers dreamed of having new clothes for a special occasion. It would take years for young ladies to accumulate some good clothes for their wedding. For the children, the Eid (religious holiday) was the primary occasion for having a new outfit. Even at school, students would wear a simple black uniform embroidered with a white collar.

No Electricity and Electrical Devices

The village had no electricity. The villagers would use the oil lamp, although even that was in limited supply. The absence of electricity would constrain village life in many ways.

Indeed, daily life was spent running around in the sunlight. The villagers would sleep and wake up early. It was considered a big shame if you were still asleep after the sunrise. This did not often happen, particularly since in the winter time, the night was long enough to sleep. Without any street lights, it was hard to go anywhere at night. Indeed, it was scary and even fearful when there was no moonlight. The fear was not because of harm from a human but from wild animals. In the winter, wolves and foxes would visit the village quite often to look for food. Many children would be scared of the possibility of being on the menu for them.

Of course, having no electricity meant having no modern appliances. No washing machines. No refrigerator. No stove. No dishwasher. No vacuum cleaner. No iron. No microwave oven. No electrical devices, whatsoever. The villagers would clean clothes by hands. They would cook food by burning wood. They would sweep the house by hand broom. They would wash the dishes by hand. Of course, they would wear clothes without ironing.

In short, what we consider to be absolute necessities in modern life were absent in the lives of the villagers. Of course, not having electricity and electrical devices were a great hardship. Having them is a great convenience. Again, it is hard to claim that in the long-run the villagers who were deprived of those necessary appliances were less happy than those who had them. While the villagers would adapt to the hardship, those who had them would take them for granted and lose the positive feeling associated with comfort which comes with the use of those devices.

No Toilet

There was no toilet in the village. The toilet culture arrived with in-house running water and electricity. I still do not know why it took such a long time for the villagers to develop a toilet. After all, it was a necessity due to human nature. Perhaps, the lack of running water was a good excuse. However, it was still possible to have a primitive form of toilet. In my understanding, there were a few reasons for not having a toilet culture.

First, was ignorance. The villagers did not know how to build a toilet. For centuries, they learned from their forefathers how to live without a toilet. They did not inherit a toilet culture. No one was urging them to come up with one. I assume that at least some villagers were aware of the existence of toilet culture through their exposure while traveling near towns. It seems that the villagers were used to live without a toilet. It was not an absolute necessity for them.

Second, they did not feel the urge to build a toilet because they could still maintain a degree of privacy within their relatively large yards. The houses were not packed together as we see in modern cities. Third, they would use the animal barn as a substitute toilet. Since most homes had a barn, they would not feel the need to build a separate toilet. In a sense, the barn was a shared toiled for humans and animals. Fourth, there was plenty of public lands that could be used as a toilet.

For me, the toilet becomes a great proxy to assess social and economic development. I consider four types of toilets as proxies for four stages of development. Ala-Kaynarca toilet, named after my village, is where the entire land is a toilet. It is an indication of a lazy and unproductive society. Ala-Turka toilet is a Turkish toilet (also known as a squat toilet) with no place to sit. It is a sign of transition from agriculture to industrial society. Ala-Franga toilet has a seat. It is the product of an industrial society. The Ala-Japanese toilet is the one that comes with an automated cleaning system. It is a sign of an information society.

Life without any toilet was very inconvenient, particularly for ladies. Ironically, the villagers were flexible enough to get used to such a life. Even though having an in-house toilet is a big jump for the quality of life, it is hard to argue that those who did not have it were less happy. Again, the adaptation principle almost equalizes those who have with those who do not.

No Market and No Money

In the early years of my village life, there was no store in the village. Therefore, there was no need for money. Life was self-sufficient. The villagers were earning their livelihood from raising domestic animals and farming. Life was quite routine and predictable. People would work in spring and summer to store food for themselves and their animals during the long winter, which lasts five to six months. They would stock up on necessary food such as cheese, flour, potatoes, onion, dried vegetables, and legumes for the winter.

There were no money-based transactions. Instead, it was a collaborative community life. People would share what they had in excess with others, with the expectation that they would get support whenever they needed it. There was no need to use money as a trusted means of exchange. The cultural trust and mutual understanding were sufficient. In a market society, money is a trusted promise of exchange in the market. If you have extra, you sell it and keep the money earned to get what you need in the future. In the village, there was no need for this since the exchange was happening at a minimal scale and with only a few trusted individuals.

Beyond altruism, the villagers would use bartering to get what they needed. For instance, in the summer, when they needed help for harvesting, they would exchange labor for labor. This was quite a common practice for cutting the hay. Those families who needed help would collaborate with each other. They would put the work in order and work for each other in sequence. Paid labor was a very alien concept to the villagers. Indeed, it was socially unacceptable to work for money. It was an insult to offer cash for the help you got from others. Being money minded was considered selfish and opportunistic.

We would have a taste of the market in the summertime. We would see traders traveling by donkey or horse from village to village to sell some essential household items such as plastic cups, metal spoons, simple clothes, etc. Indeed, the gypsy was instrumental for introducing a simple market mechanism into village life. They would also sell some items for kids such as gum and balloons.

The trade was not with money. The villagers would trade butter, cheese, or wool for anything they wanted to buy. The kids would beg their parents for eggs to exchange for gum and balloons. Later on, a small store opened in the village. However, it was in no way comparable to the kind of store we know today. There were only a few items of basic things available for sale.

The village life was in sharp contrast to modern life regarding the role of the market mechanism. While in the village, almost nothing was exchanged through the market, modern society is a market society in which almost everything is up for sale. Indeed, it seems like there is no limit to the market. You can buy respect through VIP services. You can jump to the front of a waiting line by paying a premium. You can rent a womb from a stranger to carry your baby (surrogate mother). You can live in a better jail room by paying a certain fee. You can hire foreigners as soldiers to fight for your country. In short, in a market society, you can buy or sell almost anything through the market mechanism. Therefore, money is supremely important, but never sufficient. As Arthur Schopenhauer said, "Wealth is like sea-water; the more we drink, the thirstier we become."

No Car

There were no private cars in the village. Only one minivan provided services for a fee. The minivan would go to the town in the very early morning and come back in the late afternoon. People would pay a fee for a trip to the town. Given that the villagers had minimal monetary income, it was quite a luxury to take such a trip. People would generally travel to do annual shopping for basic food or to seek necessary health treatment. In the winter, snow would block the road, and there would be no transportation for weeks, even months.

The villagers used ox carts for transporting hay, wheat, wood, etc. It took a long time for villagers to adopt horse carriages; they were faster, but not affordable. The horse was an excellent means of personal transportation. Indeed, having an expensive horse was a sign of great wealth. The elites would change their horses often to keep up with their status.

For children and low-income individuals, the donkey was the means of transportation. Compared to horses, the donkey was slower but cheaper. People would dream of getting a good horse once they became rich.

Of course, transportation is a crucial catalyst in modern life. The fast and cheap movement of people and goods has reshaped human life and relationships. The distance has become shorter and shorter as transportation gets better and better. The entire world becomes like a village in which people, goods, services, and news are exchanged at an increasing speed every day. Indeed, the enormous development in transportation brings excellent comfort to humanity by fulfilling some basic needs. However, it is hard to claim that we are happier because we have luxuries cars.

No Healthcare Service

There was no hospital in the village. Indeed, there was no healthcare whatsoever. The villagers would receive an annual visit from the nearby town for vaccination. Most kids would play hide and seek when they saw the vaccination team. The hospital visit was an unusual concept for the villagers. Most of them would never visit a hospital in their life. Of course, life expectancy was low due to the difficulty in seeking modern treatment. They would use some natural healing practices to treat any disease. They would sometime get deadly wrong. For instance, they would cover up a patient with a very high fever since the person would feel cold and ask to be covered. They had no idea that they should uncover the patient and even use a cold shower to reduce fever. Indeed, this was the leading cause of high infant mortality.

In case of emergency, it was hard for people to get to the hospital in the town due to the lack of transportation. One fake doctor used to serve several villages. He did not have any medical degree. During his military service, he learned how to give a shot. That was all he knew. He would buy some painkiller injections from the pharmacy in the town. Whenever there was a severe case, he would be invited to give a treatment. He was a great example of the placebo effect since he was giving the same medicine to everyone. For the villagers, when they were great pain, some medicine was always better than nothing.

It is important to note that life in the village was relatively free from many health problems of modern times. People would eat organic food. Obesity was an extremely rare phenomenon. The air and water were very clean since there was no industrial pollution. For that reason, the need for healthcare services was relatively limited. However, it is evident that life with access to modern healthcare services is much better since it is hard to live a life without disease or injury. It is also apparent that modern medicine reduces human suffering and extends life expectancy at birth. However, it is hard to claim that humans are happier with better healthcare services.

No Education beyond Elementary School

There was no schooling beyond elementary. Even elementary education was nothing but a language school. The native language of the villager was Kurdish. The medium of instruction was Turkish. Kids would begin schooling not knowing any Turkish. They had no opportunity to practice their foreign language other than interacting with teachers. Since all students were equally ignorant of Turkish, they would speak Kurdish with each other. Teachers would follow the curriculum, which was prepared for a native Turkish speaker. Students mostly would hate school because it took so much time for them to understand what was going on. Most kids would end up barely learning Turkish by the time they finished elementary school. They would learn only minimal things. Since there was no school beyond elementary in the village, they would soon forget whatever they learned. Indeed, the villagers would consider the school as a waste of time. For them, education had no real return. The opportunity cost for schooling was very high. They would not send their kids to school if it were not mandatory.

The village life was simple. There was no need to be a genius to learn and maintain living conditions. Unlike the industrial and information society, the villagers did not need schooling to raise a new generation. Kids would learn the culture and necessary life skills through observation and parental guidance. The villagers would live their entire lives with minimal knowledge. The primary source of knowledge was limited to life experience. Therefore, the elderly were considered more knowledgeable because they had more life experience. Indeed, it was culturally disrespectful for a youngster to speak in front of the elderly since they were considered relatively ignorant. There was no means of gaining knowledge other than personal experience or listening to the life stories of the elderly.

In short, village life was full of deprivation. People were deprived of having, doing, being, and loving. However, they were mostly content with their deprivation. Indeed, they were generally happy with their conditions. For many, ignorance was indeed bliss. For me, that was not acceptable. I did not want to die in the deprivation. I was not satisfied with my deprived life conditions as I became aware of the lives of those who had more. I also wanted to achieve greater happiness through having, doing, being, and loving. That is how my lifelong journey for happiness began.

Chapter 2

Searching for Hedonic Happiness through Having

"Contentment is natural wealth, luxury is artificial poverty."
—**Socrates**

Introduction

Perhaps every happiness journey begins with having. As soon as we gain the sense of self, we claim ownership of our toys by shouting "mine". As we grow up, we pursue more joys through more material belongings. We assume that happiness is a function of possession. We think that the more we have, the happier we would be. Thus, our happiness function is based on the expected utility from having something we like. It is a hedonic function of pleasure (utility) maximization through having more:

$$H_{h1} = U(Having)$$

13

We can't stop comparing our possessions with those of others. As we become aware of our relative deprivation, we envy those who have more. That is how the race begins. We pursue more possessions for more pleasure. We hope to realize our happiness dream once we get what we like. We think "having" what we want is true heaven. We chase more happiness through having more:

Figure 1. Hedonic Happiness through Having

My happiness journey was no different at the beginning. I was born in an agricultural society, then moved to an industrial society, then to an information society. It took three decades for me to experience what humanity has experienced over three hundred years or more. My quest for happiness through having began with deprivation and emulation but ended with achievement and disappointment. Below, I want to share my journey in the repeated "having" loop of deprivation, emulation, achievement, and disappointment, while pursuing happiness through having food, clothing, money, house, car, phone, and other technological devices.

Searching for Happiness through Delicious Food

My Food Story of Deprivation and Emulation

Like the villagers, I was not deprived of basic nutrition. What I was deprived of was the pleasure of eating a variety of food. The menu in the village was minimal. For breakfast, we would generally eat skim-milk cheese with tea and bread. Even the worst quality olive was a luxury. Whenever we made yogurt, there would be a limited amount of cream at breakfast. The other meal would rotate between potato, beans, and pasta. If available, a little meat would be added for a flavor. Of course, having a hot meal was not possible every day. We would eat yogurt with bread when there was no meal. There was no restaurant in the village. At that time, I did not know such a thing as a restaurant even existed. It was a weird idea that people would sell a meal for money. What I knew was that you should offer a free meal to those who had no food. You would not sell it to them.

It was a dream for me to eat what was not regularly available. I used to think that the rich must be extremely happy because they could eat whatever they liked. It was puzzling for me to hear that some rich people who left the village wished they could eat the village food. Honestly, I could not believe that they would miss anything from the village. As a kid, it was a dream to taste delicious food. Indeed, my food deprivation lasted until I got a job and began making money.

Bread Sandwich

I need to confess that my mom used to treat me favorably with scarce food. From the town, my dad would buy a limited amount of some luxury foods such as jam, halvah, or olives. My mom would lock them up or put them in a high place where the kids couldn't reach them. She would secretly put a small amount of halvah in a plate to quench my strong desire for a delicious taste. I still remember how tasty it was to eat halvah with bread. It was not just a dessert. It was a special meal as well as a dessert. The bread from the bakery was very rare; therefore, delicious. We would make our own tandoori bread, but the bakery baked bread was only available in the town. Once a while, my dad would buy that bread when he was in town. Since it was rare, it tasted delicious. We would make a bread sandwich by rolling the village bread around the baked bread to make sure that it would last longer. What a tasty sandwich!

Tasting Dessert for the First Time

I had minimal knowledge and taste of desserts. The village food culture did not have more than 3-5 varieties of dessert. We would eat dessert if our close relatives or we had a newborn baby. It was a tradition to cook halvah for a new mom. On rare occasions, we would have a dessert made out of milk and rice. I'll never forget when I tasted baklava (a sweet) for the first time. It was the last year of my secondary school. I had to go to a relatively big town to take the high school entry exam. I was staying at a hotel for the first time in my life. In the evening, I went outside and walked around. I saw a patisserie. I went inside and sat on a chair, waiting for the waiter to take my order. when he came, he asked me what I want to order. I responded with confidence: "I want dessert". The guy did not understand. He repeated the question. I gave the same response. He was confused. He asked a third time. I still gave the same answer. Finally, he asked me to follow him. He showed me several available desserts and asked me to choose one. I pointed to baklava. Until then, I thought a patisserie would only have baklava as dessert.

Collecting Candies

I cannot remember tasting any chocolate at all until middle school. There was no market in the village. Having any candy beyond white sugar (we used to call it tea sugar) was a dream for kids. Indeed, for many, even tea sugar was a luxury. Thankfully, the Islamic Eid (holiday) occurred twice a year. The Eid was a dream for kids. We would visit neighbors with a bag to collect candies. We had over a hundred houses in the village. On average, we would get two candies from each house, so we would make sure that we visited all the houses in the village to collect the maximum amount of sweets. We would count our candies and compare them with that of other kids to celebrate our success. We would save our bag of candies to enjoy for a few weeks. Day by day, as the bag of candies would get smaller and smaller, we would feel the pain of running out of them. We had to wait for another Eid to enjoy the pleasure of eating candies. If I had those candies now, I would not even eat them because they were low-quality candies; however, at that time, to me, they were the key to paradise.

Hungry for Fruit

The fruit was in great shortage as well. We hardly ever had any fruit. I grew up knowing only apple, orange, tangerine, melon, watermelon, grape, pear, and pomegranate, which we would have only a few times a year. For instance, during the entire summer, my dad would buy watermelon and melon only 2-3 times when he went to town. Almost always, we would have some guests when my dad would come back from the town. Therefore, our share would be no more than one slice of watermelon. Dad would also give us the rind of a watermelon. My siblings and I would make sure that no tasty part of the melon was thrown out. We would eat the melon rind almost to its green part. I still remember what my older sister used to do. She would hide her slice to eat later. My slice would be gone by then. She would eat her saved slice in front us to make us feel jealous.

I ate my very first banana when I went to college. There were no bananas in the village. I did not even see any in the town. The first time I saw a banana was when I moved to a bigger city for high school. Even then, I could not afford to buy one. I remember, one day, my roommate came home with a kilo of banana. Knowing that I had never tasted a banana, he wanted to test me to see whether I knew how to eat it. Before eating a banana, himself, he gave me one and waited for me to eat. I began eating it with its skin. Since my most familiar fruit was apple, I thought that you would eat a banana with its skin like an apple. My friend burst out laughing when he saw me eating the banana with its skin still on.

Of course, if it were rare to find fruit, it would be impossible to have fruit juice. Indeed, I never tasted any real fruit juice until I got to college. I did not even know fruit juice existed until I got to middle school. Then, I came across a fake juice. I am talking about lemonade made from lemon powder. On a hot summer day, it was a delight to drink a cup of cold lemonade. I still feel the pleasure of those rare drinks. I also experienced the taste of ice cream for the first time when I moved to the town. Even though it was inferior in its quality, it was a dream for me to lick a cone of ice cream.

My dream of a happy life with delicious food intensified when I moved to a bigger town to attend high school. There were reasons for the increased desire for delightful food. I was living at a government-owned dormitory. Though I had more food choices compared to what I used to have in the village, I had no feasible alternative if the meal was not pleasant. I remember that sometimes the meal would taste terrible. If I had money, I would buy yogurt from the nearby market and eat it with bread. Otherwise, I would kill my hunger with dry bread. The other reason was the change in my reference point. In the village, I was content with what we had because everyone in the village was living in similar conditions. In the town, I knew what I was missing. My reference point was different. Therefore, I had higher dissatisfaction with the status quo and greater aspiration to seek the pleasure of eating.

My Food Story of Accomplishment and Disappointment

I went to a hybrid high school that provided both vocational and traditional education. After I graduated, I was employed full-time while going to college. I used to work at night and go to school in the daytime. Even though it was challenging, I was grateful to have such an opportunity. It was the first time I was able to earn money and have access to delicious food. Even though I had some sleepless nights, I used to think that it was worth making such a sacrifice for the sake of money. I should mention that I was not making a lot of money.

Nonetheless, it was a big jump for me compared to the little money I had before. After completing my bachelor's degree, I found a better-paying job. As I advanced in my career, I continued to earn more. Money ceased to be an issue for me. I could afford to eat whatever I liked. I have had the opportunity to dine at the finest restaurants around the world. I have stayed at the most ultra-luxurious five-star hotels and enjoyed a wide variety of the most exquisite cuisine.

Seeking Pleasure of Variety of Food and Fruit

Indeed, the variety of food I now have access to in one month is more than what I used to have for my entire life until college. The choices we have on our breakfast table at home is no less than what is available at a five-star hotel. Real fruit juice and other soft drinks are regular companions to our daily lunch and dinner. We are never short of fresh fruit in our refrigerator at any time of the year. We can have as much meat, fish, vegetables and any other food we would like to enjoy. We have reached the level where we can have whatever we want. We have absolutely no budget constraint on food. We can afford to eat out whenever we would like. The variety of snacks we have at home is more than what a small store used to sell in our village.

I eventually had what I could not even dream of twenty years ago. I have tasted countless desserts. I have tried food from various cultures and countries. I have enjoyed the best chocolate. My dream of delicious food has been completely fulfilled. I can afford to eat and drink whatever I like. Money is not an issue at all, given my income level. However, I need to confess that my aspiration ended up giving me the ultimate dissatisfaction. I have gained access to any food I like; however, I have lost my dreamed pleasure of having them.

Seeking Pleasure of Dining at Restaurants

Obviously, it was exciting to go to a good restaurant for the first time. It was a great pleasure to taste different food. However, over time, the law of diminishing marginal utility took away from me the pleasure of eating. Indeed, according to economics, we are doomed to enjoy less and less as we have more and more. When we are hungry, the pleasure from the first slice of pizza is high. As we eat additional slices, the pleasure (utility) keeps diminishing. The decline continues to the zero utility and even below zero if we insist on eating more pizza. The law of diminishing utility applies to derived utility across different times, as well. The pleasure we get from going to a good restaurant for the first time will eventually go away as we eat out again and again.

That is precisely what happened to me. I reached the point where once incredibly delicious food began to taste ordinary. Eating at a great restaurant gave virtually no additional pleasure. I achieved almost a complete saturation when coming to food satisfaction. This doesn't mean that I do not enjoy good food anymore. Every day, I enjoy my food and drink along with my daily coffee. All I am saying is that my dream of being happy with delicious food is over. Hereby, I confess that the pleasure of eating can never bring life satisfaction. It only gives fleeting and diminishing sensual pleasure. It is not worth being a goal in life.

Pleasure Paradox: Less Pleasure with More Food

I have reached the point that I feel it is not worth living for the pleasure of eating. To me, food is no different from fuel for a car. If a vehicle consumed fuel for pleasure without fulfilling its function of getting us to our destination, I am sure we would not keep it. Similarly, if I only spend the time to eat without doing anything else, I feel that I am trashing my life. It is as if as I eat food, the food eats my life. The less time I waste eating food, the more I enjoy it. Indeed, the most delicious breakfast for me is not the one at a five-star hotel. It is a simple sandwich with tea while driving my car to work. The breakfast seems even tastier if I listen to an excellent podcast talk. That way, I do not waste my time eating. I do not schedule my time around eating. I do enjoy the food. However, it is not a drive for happiness. It does not bring life satisfaction. It is not worth being the purpose in life. It is just a flavor in overall life satisfaction.

I no longer believe that having access to a variety of food means a higher level of satisfaction. Despite the unequal and unfair distribution of income and access to food, it seems like a hidden hand is providing a relatively fair distribution of pleasure, regardless of income level. In other words, due to the law of diminishing marginal utility, it is just a matter of time before the rich lose their extra utility from having access to more variety. Indeed, one might argue that the poor might have even higher cumulative pleasure of eating compared to the rich because the poor eat only when they are starving. On the other hand, the rich are likely to eat without being hungry. Since eating while hungry gives higher pleasure, it is reasonable to assume the poor might receive a higher utility of eating.

I now understand why the rich would miss the village food. It is not baseless nostalgia. It is clear evidence that the rich lose the pleasure of eating as they gain access to various foods. They cannot reach the high satisfaction of eating that they used to have while being poor and hungry. They no longer experience hunger. Thus, they do not enjoy food that much. Furthermore, they do not consume as much energy as they did in their hard-working life in the village. Therefore, they do not feel the need for and the pleasure of eating.

Rather than acknowledging the fact that food could not bring higher life satisfaction, the rich keep trying different foods. They seek the lost pleasure at different places. They visit different restaurants. They even travel to different countries to taste different food. However, they fail to escape from the unpleasant fact that food cannot be a driving factor for life satisfaction.

Seeking sensual pleasure through eating is not limited to modern times. It is a known phenomenon historically in all affluent societies. It used to be limited to the tiny minority. The market system now makes it accessible for a relatively larger portion of society. Indeed, we have taken pleasure-seeking through eating to a new level. We are sacrificing our health while seeking satisfaction through eating and drinking. Ironically, more people are dying from overconsumption of food every year, compared to the number who are starving to death.

Searching for Happiness through Nice Clothing

My Clothing Story of Deprivation and Emulation

Naturally, clothes come after food in terms of our need and desire. We want to have clothing for functional, moral, and positional goals. During my childhood, clothing was important for both functional and positional goals. Functionally, clothing was essential in the long winter season, when we had snowy weather for almost six months. In contrast, the weather was very hot in the summertime. Therefore, having comfortable clothing was important in both winter and summer. I did not have a major problem in finding clothing that satisfied its functional goal. My deprivation and aspiration were having clothing for its image. It was a clear sign of prestige to have nice, new clothes. Indeed, it was a great source of pleasure to get new clothing.

Wearing Clothes with Patches

My parents would spend the least amount of money possible for clothes. My mom would knit socks and sweaters for the winter. Those who lived in the town or abroad would give us their used clothing. As their kids grew up, the villagers would pass on the clothes of their older kids to each other. Even the clothes of dead people would be distributed among the villagers. Indeed, my oldest uncle was the imam (a religious leader) in another town. Some people would give him the clothes of their dead. He would give them to my dad. My mom would make us wear them without telling us where they came from. I remember once my mom made pants for me out of a winter coat given to my dad. The pants did not look nice at all though they kept me warm. I was looking forward to their wearing out, so I could get a new pair. Of course, we would not throw away worn clothes. My mom would patch any holes. It was common, though not desirable, for kids to wear clothes with patches. Indeed, some kids would even have a patch over patches.

Thus, I grew up with a strong aspiration to have clothing without patches[2]. To me, having new clothes was a great source of pleasure. I had no sense of brand. It was once in a year experience to wear something new. My dad would buy new clothes and shoes just a few days before the Eid (the celebration at the end of the month of fasting). We would not be allowed to wear them until the day of Eid. I remember that we used to keep new clothes and shoes in our bed while sleeping until the Eid. My dad bought me pajamas for the first time. Not for wearing at night. They were to wear like a suit in the daytime. I wore them and visited my aunt. I felt embarrassed when she laughed at me walking around in pajamas.

Wearing Black Rubber Shoes

I have many shoe stories. For the winter, we used to have cheap black rubber shoes. It was not convenient, but okay. In the summer, rubber shoes were very hot. Therefore, my dad would buy us very simple and cheap plastic shoes for the summer. We had to wear our shoes until they were completely worn out. Of course, as a kid, my feet would grow as I grew. Thus, my dad had to buy new rubber shoes. He was not happy about that. I remember how he complained about the constant growth of my feet. On the contrary, I was delighted because it was a great excuse to get a new pair of shoes.

I do not remember being dissatisfied with my deprived condition. That was for two reasons. First, I was not the only one being deprived of new and fancy clothes. Everyone else in the village lived in a similar condition. Since our satisfaction largely derives from comparison with others around us, I had no reason to be dissatisfied. I would become aware of my deprivation when I saw

---

2   At that time, patching, ripping, tearing, slashing clothes was not fashionable. It was embarrassing to walk around with patched or ripped clothes. Thanks go to the hippies who first initiated this strange fashion. Though it is hard for me to understand its rationale, nevertheless, I welcome it for helping the poor to feel better. Perhaps, it brings a certain level of equality between the poor and the rich. Fashion companies use technology to make clothes with fake patches and rips. It would be even better if they purchased the authentic ones from the poor.

kids visiting from the city. I distinctly remember feeling inferior to those kids because of their appearance. The second reason for not being dissatisfied with my deprivation was the adaptation principle, which says that we get used to our living conditions over time.

My Clothing Story of Accomplishment and Disappointment

After I moved from the village to the town, I gradually began to fulfill my dream of having nice clothes and shoes. Indeed, one reason I wanted to have an education was to have an opportunity for better clothes. When I moved from the village to the town for my middle school education, my dad began getting nicer clothes for me. The upward trend continued as I moved to college. To me, being employed was an excellent opportunity to make money to buy nice clothes and shoes. I did so as I began working, though I was careful not to waste money.

Less Pleasure with Nicer Clothes

At the beginning, it was a great source of great pleasure to earn money and buy new clothes or shoes. After a while, getting new alone was not enough to make me happy. I was looking for a brand. It was only a pleasure if I knew the brand. I soon discovered that the law of diminishing marginal utility applied to clothes as well. As I was able financially to buy what I liked, I began losing the pleasure of having them. For me, the deceptive aspiration ended when I reached the level where I could afford to buy anything I wanted. Before that, I used to think that I would reach nirvana if I could get what was not affordable to me at that time. However, as I achieved a high-income level, the magic disappeared. I could buy any brand I liked. Money was not an issue for buying clothes. However, I did not get the pleasure I was looking for. I came to clearly understand that clothes are not worthy of being a goal at all. It was just a mirage. Even worse, I lost the pleasure that I used to have from buying new clothes. It became just an ordinary experience. Indeed, for me, shopping now is pain rather than a pleasure. I feel that I am just wasting my time for something that will not give me what I am after.

The Mistake of Judging People by Their Appearance

My journey to nicer clothing ended with a bitter realization. I learned that it is wrong to judge people by their outward appearance. A monkey will be perceived as an animal even if she/he wears the most expensive and fancy clothing. Similarly, a human's value is not determined by the cost or brand of his/her cloth. It is defined by inner character. I shall confess that it took me many years to come to this understanding. One related incident is indelibly etched in my memory. It was at the beginning of my graduate education in the United States. I had an appointment with my advisor to discuss my course plan. There was another person with my advisor. He was wearing what looked like very old and worn-out clothes. Given my experience in Turkey, I thought that he must be a cleaning guy in the department. While we were discussing the courses, he would also intervene from time to time. I was quietly wondering to myself, "What does this guy have to do with my courses?" Anyway, we settled on the course plan with my advisor. A week after, I was at my first class waiting for the professor to come. I was shocked when I saw the cleaning guy appear again. He was my professor. I was even more surprised when I learned that he had a doctoral degree from Stanford University. This incident was a turning point for me. I realized that it is wrong to judge people based on their outward appearance. Similarly, it is also wrong to try to impress others with your appearance.

Actually, I think that seeking clothes and shoes to impress others is detrimental to personal happiness. It makes one be a slave to others. The sheer expectation of praise when we buy something new is a pain. We are likely to be disappointed for three reasons. First, most people do not even pay attention to what we wear. Second, even if they pay attention, it would be very brief attention, not longer than a few fleeting moments. Third, it might ignite jealousy rather than envy.

While teaching at a private college for very wealthy students, I tried to be careful about what I would wear. One day, when I wore my three-year-old year t-shirt, I felt a little bad. It was still in good shape. However, I thought that people might think that I have been wearing that t-shirt for a long time. I decided that this would be the last time I would wear it. When I went to the office, a colleague whose office was just across from mine, told me that he liked my t-shirt. He thought I had just bought it. I responded with a big laugh while remembering my thinking that morning.

In short, my journey for nice clothes and shoes ended with the realization that we cannot achieve greater life satisfaction by having better clothes and shoes. Yes, we get pleasure in fulfilling our need for protecting ourselves from cold and heat through clothes and shoes. We also enjoy comfortable, clean, and nice-looking clothes. However, if we pursue clothing to impress others, we are likely to have more pain than pleasure. In other words, it is okay to seek clothes and shoes for intrinsic needs. However, it is painful to do for extrinsic aspiration.

Searching for Happiness through Luxury Housing

My Housing Story of Deprivation and Emulation

I was born in a house that was shared by an extended family, which included grandma and grandpa in addition to an uncle with three kids. The house was around 80 square meters (861 square feet). Each family had less than 30 square meters (322 square feet), which is about the size of an average living room in the United States. I was too little to remember how life looked in such a packed house. I remember when we were kicked out of my grandpa's house. In the village, most people live with extended family. It was communal life in which all family members would work together. The grandpa would own everything until his death. It was a rare exception to live as a nuclear family. My parents were greatly concerned when we departed from the grandparents' house. My dad was afraid that he would not be able to manage the household. However, it turned out to be a great blessing. Indeed, it was my first lesson on the free market economy. As predicted by the economist, Adam Smith, my dad would work very hard once he knew that he would be the sole beneficiary of his accomplishments.

The Village House

Our new house was made from brick and cement which was built by the government after the earthquake. It was a two-floor house without any toilet since there was no running water. Each floor had two bedrooms and one small hall. We used to live on the first floor. The second floor was kept for guests. I and my two sisters and one brother lived in the hall while mom and dad lived in one bedroom. The other room was used for food storage. It contained a big storage bin for flour. At the corner of the hall, we had a small dedicated place for taking a shower. A rolling curtain provided privacy.

We had neither electricity nor any modern heater. We would use a candle and gas lamp. Thus, we had little light. Electric power came to the village when I was about to graduate from elementary school. I remember the joy of experiencing a very bright light with electricity. Indeed, for a long time, the villagers would often turn on the light in the night just to enjoy the bright light. It was a delightful feeling. Of course, it did not take too long for the villagers to get used to it.

In the winter time, heating was a big problem. We had no modern heating devices. We would use the stove for heat. We did not have coal. Like other villagers, we would burn wood and animal waste. Given the long winter season, we had to be very careful with heating. The house would get cold at night. We would wait in our bed in the morning until my mom had lighted the stove. Of course, it was a big sacrifice for her to do so on freezing days. I would dream of living in a house with no heating problem.

In the summertime, cooling the house was the problem. For three months, we would have arid weather with very high temperatures. We would move to a high plateau to take care of the animals and enjoy relatively cool weather. We would live in a tent with no secure door. I still remember how we would get wet while sleeping in the tent during rainy nights. When we returned from the plateau, our deprived house in the village would look like a palace compared to the tent. Of course, we did not have an air conditioner. We did not have even the idea of AC. We did not know it existed. Ignorance was bliss. We would accept hot as uncontrollable fact and live with it. As kids, we would use the nearby river to cool off when the temperature was very high.

For my parents, it was essential to have a nicely furnished house. They paid attention mainly to the guest floor. It was a matter of prestige for them. In the beginning, we only had a basic carpet in the guest room along with the oriental pillows covering the wall. As my dad became affluent, he would buy more furniture. I used to grow up with stories of embellishing the house.

The Town House

I lived with my uncle while attending middle school. He had a small house with three bedrooms. Compared to the house in the village, it was like a palace. It had running water, a toilet, and electricity. Even more importantly, it had a TV. It was the first time I had been exposed to a TV. It was a fantastic experience even though it was only black and white images. I remember how I would cry with the suffering of individuals in movies thinking it was real, not a scenario. I was not alone in feeling this way. I heard some ladies would cover themselves when they would see any man on TV, thinking he could see them.

I shared the house with ten other kids, the oldest of whom was around 18 years old. In the winter time, the stove would be on only in the hall. The rooms would be used only for sleeping. I was pleased to live in such a house. The alternative was to live outside during the night while taking care of sheep as a shepherd.

The Dormitory and Student House

During my high school years, I lived in a student dormitory. This time, I shared a single room with ten other students. Of course, it was a little challenging to go to sleep with that many people. However, it did not take long before it became a new normal for me. It was much better than our house in the village because it had electricity and central heating.

During my college years, I lived in a rental house that I shared with several other college students. Four individuals would share a room. In addition, we had a hall to study and chat.

In short, I was born in very deprived housing conditions. Over time, I saw big improvement. However, it was still very much deprived compared to housing expectations in modern times. I never had a private room until I got married.

My Housing Story of Accomplishment and Disappointment

Living in Rented Apartment

My housing success began with my marriage. No, I could not afford to buy a house. However, it was a big leap for me to rent an apartment alone. The apartment was small, but enough for a new family. It had two little bedrooms, one small kitchen, and a bathroom. I had to learn how to deal with the landlord. For the next ten years, I would live in five different rental houses. In Turkey, with my income, it was not possible to buy a house. Indeed, many government employees would have to work for almost their entire lives to buy an apartment. For many, having two keys (one for home and one for a car) were the ticket to a paradise-like life.

First Owned House

My house dream became a reality when I was in the United States. After completing my Ph.D., I finally had enough money to buy a humble house using a mortgage. It was at the peak of the housing market bubble. After an intense and exciting search, we purchased a brand-new single-family house in Tallahassee, Florida. The house had a big yard and a two-car garage. It is hard to describe the joy of having your own house for the first time. I would watch the clock at work for the time to go to my sweet home. Even looking at the house from the outside was a great joy. Sitting on the patio and drinking tea was better than being at the best hotel in the world.

A year after we purchased the house, its price went up by almost fifty percent. Being an economist, I had a strong feeling that we were experiencing a bubble. I did try a few times to convince my wife to sell the house. I was not successful. It was hard to give up your home and go back to a rental property. It did not take a long time before we lost money and the pleasure of having a new house.

Sadly, the law of diminishing marginal utility was applicable to the joy of housing as well. If my memory is correct, it took less than three months to barely remember that we were living in our house. After that, whenever we remembered our days of living in rental apartments, we would feel happier. Even that form of appreciation was short-lived, though the attachment was solid.

Owning Multiple Houses

As I began to make more money, we tried to buy more houses and household items to fulfill our life-long dream. I began realizing my dream of buying furniture and household items as I began making more money. I remember that when I first moved to the United States, I would check "yard sales" over the weekend to find cheap used items. Now, I was able to buy anything I liked for my house. I reached a point where money was not an issue to buy a house or to buy any household items we wanted.

I even purchased a summer house to use for two months. I bought a house for my two kids who were going to college. I began signing a contract as a landlord rather than a tenant. It was a tremendous success for a former shepherd. However, that success was not producing the expected life satisfaction.

In short, the quality of my life was a hundred times better than what I had when I was in the village. However, as predicted by the Easterlin paradox[3], I could not claim that my subjective well-being had increased due to the change in my living conditions. Due to the adaptation principle, I found that living in a palace or living in a poor housing condition would make no significant difference in the long-run in terms of subjective well-being. I am not saying that it would be fine for me to go back to the deprived housing condition. Of course, I would be very unhappy initially if I had to live in such a condition. However, it would be just a matter of time for me to accept my condition and move on. Thus, what I am saying is that we should not expect higher life satisfaction through the housing condition. Even if we live in a gorgeous palace, we might feel as if we are in prison if we limit our search for happiness to the hedonic dimension.

Searching for Happiness with a Brand-New Car

My Car Story of Deprivation and Emulation

I began my car journey by riding a donkey. My first dream was to ride a horse. Horses were the primary means of transportation in the village. Having a good horse was a sign of wealth. My dad had a great ambition to get a horse. He would change horses almost every year.

There was only one mini-van for public transportation. For kids, it was fun to run after that car when it came back from the town. Kids were not allowed

---

3   As discussed in chapter 11 in detail, Easterlin argued that life satisfaction does rise with
     average incomes but only up to a point. Beyond that the marginal gain in happiness declines.
     Therefore, as countries get richer, paradoxically, they do not get happier.

to get inside the car. They would race to climb on the back of the vehicle. I had the great pleasure of traveling inside that car a few times until I attended middle school in the town.

Since there was no TV in the village, I had the opportunity to see a different car whenever someone would come for a visit. Indeed, any vehicle that came to the village would be at the center of considerable attention. Kids and adults would gather around the vehicle with great envy and excitement. Touching a vehicle was a pleasant experience. My dream at that time was not about owning a car, but just riding. In the village, two individuals attempted to get a driver's license. They failed several times. Each time, they would share their stories with everyone, telling how difficult it was to get a driver's license. To me, the ultimate dream was to get a driver's license and be able to drive a car.

When I moved to the town, I began to see more cars. My uncle did not have a private vehicle, So I would walk around four km to school every day. One of our relatives had a car. He had two sons who enjoyed taking care of their vehicle. I remember how I would envy them when they washed their car. Sometimes, I would ask them to let me help wash the car. I would be unhappy when they would not give me the opportunity to have the pleasure of washing the car.

There was no big bus in the town. Only mini-buses. I was curious about how they looked. One day, I went to the bus terminal and got on a mini-bus pretending to be a traveler, just to have an experience.

Everyone around me would pay attention to cars. Indeed, people were treated differently if they had a private car. It was as if your value depended on the value of your car. I should mention that cars were not expensive. They were mostly cheap used ones bought in a major city nearby.

My Car Story of Accomplishment and Disappointment

My success with the car began with the ability to rent a bike. When I was going to middle school, I was delighted that I was able to rent a bike. There was a bike rental place near my uncle's house. I would rent a bike for one hour for a few times a month. It was beyond my dreams to buy a bike because I never had that much money.

Co-Owning a Car

When I got married, I bought my first car, partnering with a friend. We were living in the same building. We both were newly married with only one kid. We could not afford to buy a car alone, so we decided to buy collectively. We would use it as needed. Of course, the partnership did not last long. We soon realized that it is hard for two families to share a car due to frequent conflicts in the schedule. I gave up my share and got my money back.

Buying a Used Car

When I moved to the United States, I realized that it was a necessity to own a car. The public transportation was extremely inefficient and limited. I bought my first car with my own money. Though it was a used car, in my judgment, it was like a brand new and precious car. I paid great attention to maintaining the car. It was liberating to move freely with your car wherever you wanted to go. In the beginning, I got great pleasure from driving the car. I never thought that one day, I would get tired of driving. To me, being in control of a car was truly empowering and entertaining.

After two years, we decided to get another car for my wife. It was a great joy for the entire family. My wife and kids would gain their independence with the second car. Over the years, as I earned more money, we would upgrade our car. It was a repetitive game. We would gain great pleasure when we purchased a vehicle. After a while, as predicted by the law of diminishing marginal utility, the pleasure would get less and less until it became zero. Rather than learning my lesson, I would wait for an opportunity to change the car. I did play this game several times. Once I realized the outcome was the same, I began contemplating about buying a brand-new car. I thought that would make a difference. At that time, it was not economically reasonable or affordable to do so. It stayed with me as a dream for several years.

Buying a New Car

When I purchased my first brand new car, I still remember the feeling of driving home from the dealer. Turning the wheel, touching the seat, even smelling the newness of the car was giving me great pleasure. I shall also confess that I was a little bit nervous due to the fear of having a car accident. Overall, it was a great experience to drive a brand-new car. I thought that the end would be different from that with the used cars. I was wrong again. Day after day, I got used to our new car. The pleasure began diminishing until it became zero. I finally realized that seeking satisfaction through owning a car took me nowhere.

In short, I grew up with the dream of touching and riding a car. Later, I experienced great joy in buying a car with a partner. Then, I managed to purchase a used vehicle alone. Finally, I earned enough money to buy a brand-new car. I reached an income level where I could afford to buy a new car every month if I wanted. However, I lost my joy of having a car. I realized that it was a mirage to seek fulfillment through buying cars. To me, changing cars was not a solution. It was just evidence that cars could not bring life satisfaction. Rather than buying an expensive car to give a false signal to others that you would be happier if you owned a better car, I decided to keep the same car for several years, telling people that I was out of this nonsense game. To me, a car is a means of transportation getting us from one point to another. It is not a means of transformation. It cannot change us. It cannot define our intrinsic value. Perhaps, it is a sign of losing innate worth. We cannot substitute our lost inner value with the value of our car.

Conclusion

My search for happiness through having hit a dead end. When I was living in extreme deprivation of something I wanted to have, I used to think that I would be happy if I have it. As I became aware of my deprivation, I began emulating those who had what I wanted to have. The intense desire to have led to hard work and accomplishments. I managed to have everything I wanted to have. I even had much more than I had wished to have. Perhaps, the only thing missing wish was the expected satisfaction that was supposed to come with having. After many trials and errors, I ended up greatly disappointed with having. After many repeated tours in the having loop, I realized that seeking happiness by having is nothing but a dead loop, as portrayed below:

Figure 2. DEAD Loop of Happiness with Having

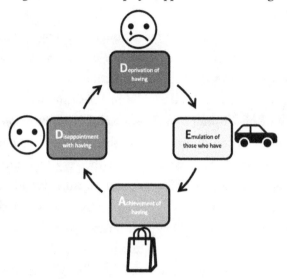

In my understanding, several factors explain this paradoxical phenomenon of the DEAD loop of seeking happiness through having.

First, the pain of hard effort to have something is almost always greater than the pleasure of achieving possession. Thus, as predicted by the hedonic treadmill, we make no progress in subjective well-being as we work harder to consume more.

Second, the law of diminishing marginal utility is applicable to all kinds of material consumption. It is just a matter of time before we take for granted what we possess.

Third, seeking possession is mostly for extrinsic aspiration which brings fleeting joy if we manage to receive praise from others. As shown by many empirical studies, the fulfillment of intrinsic rather than extrinsic aspirations is likely to increase subjective well-being.

Fourth, whenever we like something, we have to establish a certain attachment to our object of love. However, every attachment is doomed to end up with detachment. And every detachment results in certain pain. That is why the "endowment effect" predicts that we put a higher value on anything we own. Thus, we require a higher reward to compensate for the pain of detachment.

In short, it becomes clear to me through life-long experience that the problem is with the way we define happiness. It is a deadly mistake to assume that the more we consume, the happier we become.

Marginal utility is defined as the additional pleasure/benefit we receive from an additional unit of consumption. It is a well-known principle in economics that marginal utility of consumption diminishes as we consume more units. For instance, when we are hungry, we start with the very high pleasure of eating our favorite food, such as pizza. However, our pleasure diminishes as we eat an additional slice until it becomes zero. When we feel that we are completely full, we reach zero marginal utility. If we push further, we will have negative utility (disgust). In the short-run, that is due to our biological limit. We have to wait for our stomach to be empty to enjoy eating again. We get tired of eating the same thing over time. One short-term solution is to seek variety. We try different foods. However, as shown below, we argue that the law of diminishing marginal utility is also valid in the long-term as we get more opportunity to consume various things. Paradoxically, the more we consume, the less pleasure we receive.

Figure 3. Long-term Marginal Utility of Having (Consuming) Something

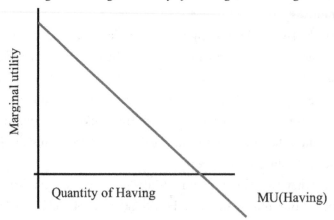

As shown above, as our overall long-term marginal utility of consumption approaches zero, our life satisfaction will also approach zero. If our happiness is based on having (consuming) something $\{H_{h1} = U(\text{Having})\}$, our marginal happiness is going to approach zero over time. We will begin seeking an alternative way to find happiness.

Chapter 3

Searching for Hedonic Happiness through Doing

"Happiness is not achieved by the conscious pursuit of happiness; it is generally the by-product of other activities."
—Aldous Huxley

Introduction

As we hit the dead end in the search for happiness through having, we might think that doing what we like would be a great complementary addition. We will expand the hedonic happiness by adding "doing" as shown below:

$$H_{h2} = U \text{ (Having, Doing)}$$

We are still in the same dimension, aiming to reach pleasure maximization. Metaphorically speaking, as we run out of gas, we refuel through fun activities. We give greater importance to pleasant life experiences in addition to material possessions. We might even think of "having" as a means for "doing" what we like. We would count and compete for more fun experiences. We hope the more we have and do what we like, the happier we will be.

My happiness journey through doing was not different. As a former part-time shepherd, I used to have the opportunity to wander around only a few mountains and nearby villages. I was living in extremely deprived conditions compared to those who had many fun experiences. As I became aware of my deprivation of doing, I envied those who had great opportunities to travel around the world, to enjoy better food, and to stay at better hotels. I began thinking that my happiness equation would be complete if it included both having and doing:

Figure 1. Hedonic Happiness through Having and Doing

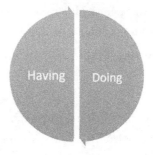

Below, I will first share my journey of seeking happiness through doing, starting from deprivation and emulation, and ending with achievement and disappointment. Then, I will discuss scientific findings on the relationship between doing and happiness.

Deprivation and Emulation Phase

Childhood without Toys

I was born in living conditions that offered extremely limited opportunities for enjoyment. As a child, I was almost completely deprived of modern toys. I never had a toy car. Instead, I remember I used to make a wheel out of wood or leftover watermelon skin. I never had a bike. I used to ride a donkey. I never owned a toy weapon. I used to make a bow and arrow from a stick. The only modern toys I remember owning were a balloon and a plastic flute.

Some kids in the village had a few simple plastic toys. Overall, spending money on toys was not an option for any villager. I never saw any children's entertainment park until my high school years. I did not know such places even existed until my childhood was almost over.

Of course, that does not mean that I did not enjoy my childhood. Indeed, I had a very happy childhood. Like other kids in the village, we would make toys out of a variety of things. However, we had a strong desire for modern toys. Whenever a kid from the town would visit the village, we would look at his/her toys with great envy.

We played outdoor games almost every day. Though I was not a great player, I used to enjoy playing soccer. The problem was that I did not have a ball. Actually, in the village, only two or three individuals could afford to buy a football. We had to please them if we wanted to play with their football. If they got angry for any reason, the game would end abruptly. They would take their ball and leave.

Life without a TV

When I was born, there were no iPods, no smart devices, and no PCs. Television was the main entertainment tool. We had no TVs in the village. I never watched TV until my middle school years while living with my uncle. Of course, it was fascinating to watch movies and news even though they were all in black and white. Color TV broadcasting became available when I was in high school.

In the village, we had two modern entertainment tools: a radio and a tape player. Most homes had the former, while only wealthy individuals had the latter. I remember that one guy who owned a tape player would play music very loudly to let the entire villagers enjoy it freely. Of course, for both devices, it was difficult to keep up with the cost of getting batteries. I never went to a theater during my childhood. Even later on, it was an extremely rare experience to go to a movie.

No Travelling

I never traveled beyond 20 km from the village where I was born, until my school years. I remember that when I was little, I imagined that the entire world consisted of only several villages around us. I told myself if I went to the top of the surrounding mountain, I could touch to the sky. I had no idea that our planet is like a grain of sand in the universe. Later on, when I heard about the existence of other cities, I had a great desire to go there. Indeed, it was a joy to listen to stories from those who visited other places. Toward the end of my elementary school years, a villager opened a little store by converting a room of his house to a market. I remember seeing a poster of the Istanbul Bosporus Bridge posted on his door. It was amazing to imagine a bridge over the sea. To me, it seemed like a life-changing experience to visit such a place.

No Vacation

Of course, I never had a vacation until my college years. I had never even heard the word "holiday" until my middle school years. Therefore, I never stayed at a hotel, except once, until my college years. I stayed with a relative on the rare occasions that I visited a place. It was hard for me to accept the idea of having to pay for bed and food. Also, I did not know what a picnic was, until college. To me, life was studying or working. Resting was nothing but refreshing myself for studying or working.

The first time I had a chance to go beyond my hometown was when I passed an exam to go to a publicly-funded school in the west of Turkey. I had no information about the quality of the school. The main reason that I wanted to go to that school was to have the opportunity to travel outside of my hometown. Primarily, it was to have a chance to see Istanbul. I used to hear stories about the beauty of Istanbul. I had a powerful desire to see Istanbul. The school was located in a city just beyond Istanbul. I traveled with a relative by bus to Istanbul, first. Then, I went to the town of my new school. I still remember the amazing feeling I had when we were crossing the Bosporus. I was awestruck to watch the sea and see the bridge for the first time in my life. The relative who was traveling with me was watching me while I was watching the sea and the bridge. She later reported to me and others that my mouth was literally wide open while looking at the bridge. That was a clear sign of how amazed I was at this unique experience. However, fulfilling my dream of seeing Istanbul was not the end, but just the beginning of desiring more and more.

In my childhood dream, I used to think that those kids who had modern toys and bikes were much happier. To me, those who had access to modern entertainment had no reason to be unhappy. I was thinking they lived in a paradise-like life while I was still struggling to get there. As I moved out of the village and the town, I began admiring more. That is when I started to realize what I had been missing. To me, wealthy people were much happier. They traveled. They stayed at the best hotels. They vacationed in the best places. They attended entertainment events. They ate at great restaurants. They bought what they liked. Therefore, it was evident that I needed to make money to be happy like them.

Accomplishment and Disappointment Phase

It was a great accomplishment to move out of the village in which I was born. At that time, most people would be born and die in the village without traveling beyond a few villages nearby. However, it was still a partial accomplishment. When I went to college, I had the opportunity to have more experience of doing what I liked. I began traveling to some cities. I would visit museums and zoos. I would take a brief vacation to cities with beaches. The life for me was much richer than what I used to have in the village. However, it was not giving me great satisfaction I was looking for. Life was still a familiar game. I would get excited about a new experience for the first time. The excitement would die out after repeating two or three times. For instance, when I first visited a zoo in Istanbul, I was truly amazed at the animals that I saw for the first time. It was a fantastic experience. Later on, when I visited the same place a second and third time, the pleasure died out almost entirely.

Each time, I would hit a dead end in seeking satisfaction through individual experience, I would begin looking for another one. My real success (and failure) started with having a job. As I made more money while advancing my career, I would realize more and more of my dreams related to doing something pleasant. I would go to a good restaurant more often. I would travel. I would go on vacation. After getting my bachelor's degree, I started dreaming of traveling outside Turkey. For me, the only way to have such an experience was through education. Since I did not speak English, I set a goal to learn English, mostly through self-study. I passed an exam for a scholarship to do my Ph.D. in the United States.

First International Trip

I still remember my first experience when I landed in New York. It was like moving to another planet. For the first time in my life, I saw many people of color. It was a complete cultural shock. I felt like a child while learning my way around the town with the help of a good friend. It took a few months to get used to life in the United States, from driving to shopping. I made friends with people of different color, faith, and countries. I had a Buddhist neighbor. My kids would call him "budhi uncle". I met people from China, Indiana, Pakistan, Mexico, France, etc. It was like a miniature world with people from various countries and cultures. The incredibly diverse society and culture were amazing to me.

While curious about the richness of diversity, I was also afraid of losing my own culture and identity. Thus, it took time for me to explore various aspects of the culture. I remember I made my first visit to a church after two years of invitations by a professor. Right after the visit, I sent a message to my friends encouraging them to visit a church as soon as possible. For me, it was a great experience to see similarities and differences between my religion and Christianity. Later on, I made friends from various different sects of Christianity. We also set a monthly meeting with Jews and Muslims.

At one church visit, I met a group who called themselves Free Thinkers. Though they defined themselves as atheists, they would have a weekly meeting at a church. That was quite a strange phenomenon for me. I met with their group leader and made friends with him. For over three years, we would meet every weekend at the edge of a lake in the downtown area to engage in intellectual discourse. I published four books in Turkish covering our debates.

Traveling around the World

Again, the adaptation principle ruled. I began taking granted what I was experiencing. My life was back to routine. I lost the excitement and pleasant feeling of being in the United States. I started dreaming of visiting other countries. For me, as an academician, attending conferences had a dual purpose: sharing my ideas with colleagues and discovering new places and culture. Even though I did not travel beyond 20 km from my birthplace until my school years, I ended up visiting over 20 countries in five continents in a few years while giving talks at conferences and workshops. I had the opportunity to stay at luxury five-star hotels. I visited almost all the major touristic cities around the world including Orlando, San Francisco, Paris, London, Venice, Tokyo, Toronto, New York, Kuala Lumpur, Seoul, Berlin, Melbourne, etc. I went to the best museums around the world. I saw whatever movies I thought it was worth to watch at the theater. I cruised on a private yacht. I had almost every kind of experience I found to be morally right.

Disappointment with Traveling Experience

I found completely different facts than what is shared on social media. Shared pictures and stories were not consistent with my experience. I did not want to lie to the world that I had great success and amazing life experiences. Yes, it was quite a success to move from the very bottom income level to the very top level. With money, I had the opportunity to experience what wealthy people would do. However, I did not want to be an actor giving false signals to everyone as if my enriched life experience brought me greater happiness. I did not want to tell people that I was very happy because of being able to travel to many countries, experience many things that are portrayed as happy events on media every day. From personal experience, observation, and reading, I would like to confess that none of the great experiences I later managed to have brought me what I was hoping for. Indeed, in the beginning, it was thrilling to have such fun experiences. However, the end of the story was very disappointing. I want to share three incidents as an example.

Sharing to Deceive

Once, a friend invited me to visit the deep sea on his yacht for fun. Initially, I rejected the offer. When he insisted, I thought that it would be rude if I did not go. At that time, I was already convinced that pursuing such pleasures is nothing but a waste of time. Thus, I decided to make the trip reflective in order not to waste my time. I was observing several individuals on the yacht. As we went along, they engaged in some activities such as swimming, fishing, and eating. I noticed that their facial expressions were completely different when they posed for a photo. If I had not been with them, I would have assumed that they had a delightful experience during their trip. In reality, they were posing happily only when they were taking a picture. The picture was utterly deceptive because it was telling others that they were happy because of having such a great day on the yacht. The truth of the matter was contrary. It was just an ordinary experience for them. No observable difference in their happiness given their repetitive experiences.

Losing the Joy of Five-Star Hotels

The second example is about my experience with hotels. I rarely stayed at a hotel before moving to the United States. There, I would choose a hotel based on price and cleanliness. Until recent years, it was not economically affordable to stay at five-star hotels. I used to think that staying at a five-star hotel would make a big difference. I was delighted when I finally made enough money to stay at such a hotel. Like all life experiences, initially, it was new and different. Particularly, having an open buffet breakfast with hundreds of items to choose from was a surreal experience. However, the magic did not last long. After several times, staying at a five-star hotel became no different from staying at a nice one-star hotel. When I began losing the pleasure of staying at the five-star hotel, I thought that something was wrong with me. I checked with my wife and kids and realized that they had the same reaction. Of course, if we have to stay at a one-star hotel, we recognize the differences. We all like staying in a clean and comfortable hotel. However, staying at a luxury or ultra-luxury hotel makes absolutely no difference once it becomes a regular experience. The adaptation principle takes away the initial positive feeling. Over time, you get used to the standards and receive no extra pleasure.

Once I was staying at an ultra-luxury hotel as an invited speaker by a university. All services at the hotel were exaggerated to the maximum. The hotel had perfect facilities for various activities. I was curiously examining the facial expressions of individuals staying at the hotel, trying to see whether they were happier than those who remained in a low star hotel. I could not find any difference. I argue that if we survey regular attendees of low and high star hotels, we will see no difference between them regarding daily subjective well-being during their stay.

Losing the Joy of Entertainment

The third example is about visiting theme parks. I remember how amazing it was to visit Sea World in Orlando for the first time. It was like a tour deep down into the ocean. It was a great experience to see so many sea animals up close. It was a fantastic experience to watch the shows. As a family, we were all excited. We decided to come back soon. We knew that we should take a break before the second visit. Two years later, we went back; we barely enjoyed the experience. The magic was gone. It was just boring repetition to a great extent.

Indeed, I have moved from complete deprivation to full saturation in terms of many life experiences. As I mentioned before, I never had a picnic in my life until my college years. I now have the opportunity to have a picnic whenever I want to. However, I almost completely lost the pleasure of having a picnic just for fun.

Similarly, I had no experience of eating at a good restaurant until I was employed. Now, I could eat at any restaurant I want. However, I do not feel excited to go to a restaurant only to enjoy delicious food. I feel as if the food is eating my life rather than the other way around. I need to have other reasons for being with family or friends besides eating to enjoy my food.

Once, as a reviewer for the Journal of Happiness Studies, I reviewed a research paper on the impact of vacation on subjective well-being. The study's finding was contrary to general expectations. It revealed that those who vacation at luxury places end up being less satisfied once they are back compared to others. The author (s) had difficulty to explain this paradox. In my view, the reason behind that phenomenon is that those who go to luxury tourist destinations are likely to encounter people who are wealthier. They will engage in mental comparison and feel bad about what they have. On the other hand, those who visit a place with people who are less fortunate in terms of economic wellbeing will feel better and appreciate what they have.

Conclusion

I got almost all of my wishes in terms of fun experiences. I have traveled almost everywhere I want to see. I have eaten at any restaurant I chose. I have stayed at the best hotels in the world. However, I could not find lasting life satisfaction in any of those experiences. My journey of seeking satisfaction through doing something was no different from the previous one. It became clear to me that adding "doing something you like" to the happiness equation leads to the same dead end: disappointment and dissatisfaction.

Figure 2. DEAD Loop of Happiness with Doing Fun Things

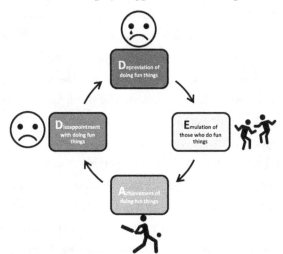

What I have learned is that it is not possible to find lasting life satisfaction in doing something you like for several reasons:

First, it is not that we do not want to have a good life experience. My argument is that we pursue life experience for need fulfillment and image. The former does bring certain satisfaction although it diminishes when repeated, while the latter is ultimately detrimental to life satisfaction. For instance, it is our psychological need and desire to pursue clean and comfortable hotels. We enjoy staying at a nice hotel while traveling or vacationing. However, the initial extra enjoyment we receive is not sustainable. The joy we receive from experience does not bring the expected fulfillment in life.

Second, it is the adaptation principle that causes diminishing marginal utility from life experiences. It does not matter how great our experience is; it will eventually become an ordinary one. That is true for almost all life experiences including visiting a great museum, going on the best safari tour, and staying at the best hotel.

Third, if we pursue life experience to hear praise from others by sharing a perfect picture on social media, that is detrimental to our subjective wellbeing. Many studies have indicated that seeking satisfaction through extrinsic aspiration is not possible.

Fourth, as we enrich our life experiences, we will discover a commonality among them. Therefore, we will not gain the expected additional satisfaction. For instance, if we are a frequent traveler, we will soon notice that it is not worth it to travel a thousand kilometers for something that you have nearby. It is hard to claim there is a big difference between beaches, lakes, gardens, scenes, zoos, and so on. They all have a lot in common. The more one travels, the more one becomes aware of this commonality.

Fifth, as we pursue luxury life experiences, we are likely to run into those who are more fortunate than us in terms of their wealth and positions. Since it is hard to avoid comparing our life with theirs, we will end up being less satisfied with what we have. Thus, it does not make sense from the perspective of subjective wellbeing to stretch our means to have expensive life experiences.

Sixth, even though we get certain pleasure in having different life experiences, we will not be satisfied with that. We will eventually realize that doing different things for the sake of recording and sharing nice pictures in our memory or in the memory of a digital device could not be the end goal in life. It is ultimately meaningless to live a life for taking pictures rather than understanding the meaning of life. If we liken life to a meaningful book with amazing pictures, it is entertainment for a child just to enjoy the pictures. However, as an adult, we could not be satisfied with images alone. We want to read the text as well, to learn the meaning. In short, pursuing perfect pictures through different life experiences is a childish way of seeking satisfaction. It cannot bring ultimate satisfaction to a grown up.

As shown in Figure 3, as we gain the opportunity to seek happiness by doing fun things, our combined marginal utility will shift to the right. In other words, we will receive higher marginal utility compared to our utility from just "having" alone. However, we cannot overcome the law of diminishing marginal utility.

Even though we manage to shift the line, we are still living in the one-dimensional hedonic level. As we realize our diminishing satisfaction while running down along the curve, we will try different fun activities to move up our marginal utility. This will help in the short-run. The more we gain an opportunity for having (consumption) and doing (fun things), the less pleasure we derive from them due to the diminishing (down-sloping) nature of marginal utility.

Figure 3. Long-term Marginal Utility of Doing Fun Things

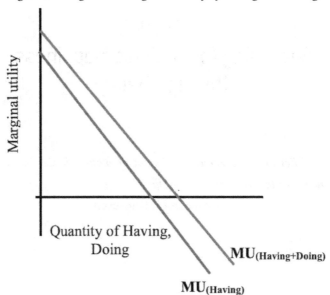

As we realize our marginal utility from having and doing is doomed to approach zero over time, our life satisfaction will also approach zero. In other words, our marginal happiness based on the function of H_{h2} = U (Having, Doing) is going to approach zero over time:

$$\Delta H_{h2} \rightarrow 0 \text{ as } \Delta U \rightarrow 0$$

As we approach the dead end in our quest for happiness with having and doing, we will become desperate to search for an alternative way.

Chapter 4

Searching for Hedonic Happiness through Being

"Happiness lies not in the mere possession of money; it lies in the joy of achievement, in the thrill of creative effort."
—Franklin D. Roosevelt

Introduction

As discussed in the previous chapters, we are almost certain to go through the DEAD loop while pursuing lasting happiness through "having" and "doing". As we experience disappointment with having and doing, we will simultaneously search for the missing element in our quest for lasting happiness. As we realize the inner joy of gaining the respect and recognition of other individuals, we will refuel at the "being" station, aiming for lasting happiness. We want to gain the respect of others by being something through some accomplishments. Though we are still on the hedonic dimension, we will expand our happiness equation by adding being (B) as a third element:

H$_{h3}$ = U (Having, Doing, Being)

My happiness journey through being began at almost the very bottom. As I grew up, I realized that I was "Mr. Nothing". Except for my parents, I felt I had no value in the eyes of others. I was no different from a bird or a plant in gaining respect and recognition. I fought hard to climb from the very bottom to the very top of gaining reputation and respect in the eyes of others. I thought I would reach complete happiness if I succeeded in becoming something important. Thus, I intensified my search for happiness with having, doing, and being:

Figure 1. Hedonic Happiness with Having, Doing, and Being

Deprivation and Emulation Phase

Dream of being Something
I began realizing my deprivation of being when I was in elementary school. I had the same status as everyone else in the village. I would become aware of my deprivation whenever we had a visitor from the town. The explicit respect and envy shown by the villagers to those wealthy visitors were a clear message that I was living in a deprived condition. I remember how inferior I would feel when I played with those relatively rich kids from the town. Everyone in the village openly accepted their inferiority to those in the town. They would show utmost respect to any high-ranking government official visiting the village. I remember once the top government administrator of the town was going to visit. It took a week for the villagers to prepare for the visit. They prepared a special feast for the visitors. Everyone was talking about the honor of having such a visit. For

me, it was a great blessing to see the honored guest from a far distance. I had no dream of reaching such a position. My dream was to have an opportunity in the future to directly serve such people of high position. I remember once I was pouring water on the hands of a guest. His hands were much whiter than mine. That was a sign of superiority in my mind. I received great pleasure in serving such a person. At that time, I had no idea that black people even existed. In my world, there were only brown and white people. My childish theory was that as you became something, your skin got lighter. Due to my feeling inferior to those visitors with bright skin color, I remember that I used white powder to see whether I could change the color of my skin.

Shepherding vs. Schooling

The visitors were both a reminder of what I was missing and a source of inspiration for what I could be. It became clear to me that I had to leave the village to gain wealth and/or a governmental position to attain high status in the eyes of people. Otherwise, I was going to die as a Mr. Nothing in the village. Education was the only means to be a Mr. Something. I worked very hard and managed to complete my elementary education with an honors degree. My teachers all agreed that I had great potential. The problem was that we had no school beyond elementary in the village. I had to move to the town for further education, but my parents were not willing to support me for that. My dad barely completed elementary school while my mom was a dropout from the third grade. The story I was told was that my dad used to bribe his teachers with fresh eggs and milk to get a passing grade. Thus, they had no appreciation for education.

Furthermore, my dad was a dealer trading livestock. For him, the opportunity cost of sending me for further education was too high. In addition to the cost of schooling, he would have to hire a full-time shepherd to do the work I would have done. As a business minded person, he did not see any value of investing in my education. There was no success story before me. Indeed, several kids before me got a high school diploma but had no career. Thus, from his perspective, it would be a complete waste of resources to send me to the town for further education. For him, this was just a simple cost and benefit analysis. The opportunity cost of my education was way above the expected benefit.

For me, it was a dream to have an education. I used to work as a part-time shepherd during my elementary education. It was not a pleasant experience and I did not want to be a full-time shepherd. The career trajectory my parents planned was clear. I would work as a shepherd in the beginning. Once my daddy became rich, I would begin shifting my career by helping him as a livestock dealer. I did not like that. I had a strong desire to be something through education. I had one advantage to realize my dream: I had an uncle who used to live in the town. He did not have an education beyond elementary; however, he had spent some time working in Germany. Thus, he had the first-hand experience of the high value of education. He encouraged everyone in the village to educate their kids. Whenever he would visit the village, he would ask about my performance at the school. He would tell me that he would take me to the town for further education if I got good grades.

Running away from home to the school

My uncle was my only hope for an education. During the summer, right after my graduation, I insisted that my dad take me to the town. I was supposed to enroll during the summer before school began. I had to go to the town with him to enroll in middle school. My dad went to the town a few times in the summer. Each time, I would ask him to go for the enrollment, he would find an excuse to postpone it to the next time. The summer was almost over, and I knew that he was not going to take me to the town. I began thinking about an alternative way of getting there. A single mini-van provided transportation from the town every day. The villagers would go in the morning and return in the evening. Interestingly, my dad fought with the owner of the mini-van. He would not get in his car. He would walk to the nearby village to use their public transportation.

My dad was going to town again. It was my last chance. I asked him to take me with him. He again came up with an excuse. In the early morning, he left the village on foot to the nearby village. I made an alternative plan. I secretly got into the car from our village to run away from home. I went to my uncle in the town and asked him to enroll me in middle school. He was pleased to help me. Without delay, he took me to a photo studio to take my picture for the registration. After the photo was taken, I fainted at the studio. They took me to a doctor. I knew what the problem was, but I was too shy to tell them. At the clinic, I fainted again while having my first intramuscular injection. When I gained consciousness, they took me to a restaurant. While drinking my soup, I thought to myself, "Here is my real medicine". I was hungry from the day before because of my runaway plan. As I was sipping my soup, I felt better and better. Despite those adversities, it was one of the best days in my life. I was very happy that I was going to have an education.

The journey of becoming something was not over. It was just starting. When I moved from elementary to middle school, I realized that I was very much behind the students in the town. I also felt that I was treated even worse due to my language and appearance. My mother language was Kurdish. I began learning Turkish in elementary school. Though I had no problem in understanding, reading, and writing, I had a very heavy accent. That was enough to be treated as inferior by native Turkish speakers.

Furthermore, my appearance clearly told everyone that I was a village boy. I had to fight hard to gain respect in the eyes of others through better performance. I had two options: 1) work hard and be successful or 2) be lazy and go back to the village and be a shepherd. Given my experience as a part-time shepherd, I felt that I had no option but to work to be successful. The first year was quite challenging. In the second year, I managed to be on the top honor list. That helped to overcome the stereotype. After that, I was no longer treated as a regular village boy. Instead, I was seen as an exception.

Studying in a room with ten kids

I stayed in my uncle's home for three years, sharing a little house with his ten kids. In the winter time, we used the main hall in the daytime. We would use the bedroom only to sleep. Thus, I had to develop a special technique to study in this very crowded family. I would lie on the ground on my stomach but propped up on my elbows and blocking my ears. The noise of kids was like background music. I never felt bothered because I was extremely appreciative that my uncle was giving me such an opportunity. Indeed, I knew some kids from the village who could not continue their education despite their enormous potential because they had no one like my uncle to support them. Even today, I feel great indebtedness to my uncle for his kind hospitality.

My hard work paid off. After three years, I passed an exam to attend a nursing high school. It was a vocational school, which would allow me to get a job as soon as I graduated. It was an excellent opportunity for me. The school was located in the far west of Turkey. I was going to travel outside my hometown for the first time. It was truly exciting. I was the first one in the village to pass this exam. This was something in the eyes of people and I began earning some respect. After the summer break, I moved to the new town and started high school. Once again, I was reminded that I was nothing. This time, it was students from the western part of Turkey who treated me like a village boy. The initial mistreatment is still fresh in my memory. I was sharing a bunk bed with a boy from the west of Turkey. He spoke very fluent Turkish and dressed well. I tried to be friends with him, but he avoided me due to my broken Turkish and appearance. I had to study even harder to overcome the bias.

In short, from a very early age, I learned my lesson well. I thought one of the keys to happiness was to gain recognition in the eyes of others by being something. To me, the road to success for recognition and wealth was possible through education. Thus, as a Mr. Nothing, my entire educational journey became a very long race to catch with up those who were a Mr. Something.

Accomplishment and Disappointment Phase

My success story began with completing middle school with an honors degree and passing an exam to pursue my high school education at a vocational school for nurses. The journey took almost three decades until it hit a dead end. At every stage, I would set a dream and work very hard to succeed. I would be thrilled when I achieved my goal; however, this happiness would be very short-lived. After each disappointment, I would begin another race by setting another goal. Thus, for almost thirty years, I raced toward the ultimate success.

Attending Nursing School

In high school, my dream was to graduate with an honors degree and go to the best college. The problem was that my school was a vocational one. The curriculum was designed to provide education for nurses, not for those preparing for the college entrance exam. We were given assurance that we would be employed as a nurse as soon as we graduated. That was the main reason I was there. The cost to my parents was zero as it was a fully-funded governmental school. Furthermore, once I graduated, I would have a job to support myself and even help my parents. The problem was that it was not my dream job. I did not want to retire as a nurse. My only option was to study hard to pass the nationwide college entry exam to get a college education. The exam was very comprehensive and competitive. I had to compete with nearly one million students around the country. I could go to my dream school if my score was in the top one percentile. I had to keep up with subjects that were not covered at my school.

Dreaming of getting to College

I did study very hard for three years, dreaming of my success in the exam. I literally had a dream of taking the exam before even doing so. Actually, I have a funny memory of this exam. I was staying with a good friend in the last few days before the exam, which used to be given once a year. I was doing a final review to make sure that I would be ready for the most important exam in my life. One night, I dreamed that I overslept and missed the exam. Of course, it was devastating. I woke up with that shock. I checked the clock; it was 10 am. The exam had started at 8 am. I ran to the other room and found my friend relaxing. I began complaining and blaming him for not waking me up. I was furious at him. He was shocked and puzzled trying to understand why I was angry. Once he realized that I was complaining because I thought I missed the exam, he burst out laughing. He pointed to the calendar and reminded me that the exam date had not arrived yet.

My hard work and obsession with the exam paid off. I was the first one in our village who passed the exam and went to college. I did better than 99 percent of all students who took the exam with me. With that score, I did manage to get into the college of my first choice. Of course, the joy of success was extraordinary. I celebrated my victory with my parents, relatives, and friends. It was a surreal experience. However, it did not last long. Indeed, the high moment lasted only a few minutes. The diminishing positive feeling continued for a few more days;

then, it disappeared almost completely. Apparently, it was not worth working painfully hard for three years just to experience an intense pleasure for three minutes. Thus, it would not make sense to go through such experience for pleasure maximization. I had other expectations beyond a pleasant feeling.

Working at night while studying in the daytime

I was working at a major hospital at night and attending classes in the daytime during my college years. I had many sleepless nights. However, I was happy with my conditions. Actually, I was thinking myself lucky to have an opportunity to work and attend college. I had seen many students struggling to survive with very little money. I did not have a financial problem. I explored my career options and decided to pursue an academic path. I realized that I needed to learn English and receive my graduate education in the United States or the United Kingdom, But I did not have the financial means to do so. I completed my bachelor's and then master's degree while exploring opportunities to go abroad. I could not find any. I began my doctoral degree in education at two different universities at the same time. I completed course requirements for both programs before passing an exam to get a scholarship to pursue my third doctoral degree abroad. Later on, I submitted my thesis and completed a first doctoral degree in Turkey while I was in the United States studying for my third doctoral degree.

The joy of getting my first Ph.D.

It was a great success to be among a very limited number of individuals to earn a full scholarship for graduate education in the United States. Education was not only a means for me to see the towns beyond my village, but it was also a means for me to see the world beyond my country. I believe I was the first one in our hometown to have such a great opportunity. I received praise from many people for having such great success. I kept working hard to keep up with the increasing expectations of me. I completed not one but two doctoral degrees. Again, I was a very successful student. The end outcome in terms of pleasure was always the same. I would suffer the pain of hard work for years to experience a few moments of pleasure. I remember the feeling of getting my graduation cap and taking a picture after four years of tough works for my second doctoral degree. Though I felt an intense sense of joy and pride to be a Ph.D. holder, I could not stop myself from asking the following: was it all for the sake of taking a picture?

Educational success was not sufficient for me. I was not satisfied to just pursue a higher degree. I was always looking for something else to gain higher satisfaction. During my college years, I became involved in the media. I worked at a radio station for a few years, hosting guests to discuss different issues. I also worked at a TV station in a similar capacity. Those experiences gave me direct knowledge of how to build my image and gain recognition in the eyes of others. Initially, it was a terrific experience. I still remember how exciting it was to have live broadcasting in the early days of my broadcasting career. It was as if the whole world were listening. Getting positive feedback from the audience was a great source of joy. Interestingly, over time, I got used to the experience. It became just a regular event in my life. I no longer felt excitement while being on the show.

The joy of being an author

While pursuing my doctoral degree in the United States, I began writing books. It was a fantastic experience to have my first book published. I was a great reader and envied many writers. It was a dream for me to be a writer one day. Publishing my very first book through a major publisher in Turkey was a big success. The book sold thousands of copies in two years. I would check my email every day to see if there were any messages from the readers. The publisher would organize book signing events at book fairs. That was another fantastic experience in my life. I would go to the event hoping to get many readers. I would experience the joy of being a known author and the fear of not getting enough attention. Then, my second book was published. Though it was not like the first time, it still gave me some joy to publish another book. As I kept publishing a book every year or so, my pleasure and excitement diminished. After publishing five books, the magic of being an author completely disappeared. It became just another ordinary life event with almost no extra joy.

Being a former shepherd with two Ph.Ds.

Though getting a Ph.D. in my third language was not easy, it did not take long to realize that the degree was just the beginning of the race. I was already a doctoral candidate in Turkey when I decided to move to the United States. Thus, I decide to complete my unfinished Ph.D. I wrote a second doctoral thesis and defended it with great success. I was probably the first former shepherd who managed to get two doctoral degrees. With two doctoral degrees in hand, I embarked on my academic career. I first worked as a full-time researcher at a research institute for several years. Then, I moved to a university as an assistant professor. I noticed that the race was getting harder and harder. Now, I had to either publish in good journals or perish as a poor academician. I would feel horrible whenever I heard failure stories. I would feel a mix of envy and jealousy when I listened to success stories. With both great fear and hope, I began my publication journey. I would work hard for months to write a good paper. Then, I would wait to hear good news after submitting it to a journal. The first time I received a rejection was devastating. After a while, it became clear to me that success and failure was the name of the game. I would not despair if I were rejected. I would try another journal.

I eventually learned how to get several articles published. They helped me to get my title of "Associate Professor". It was a great joy to be promoted after four years of work in publishing, research, and teaching. Again, the pain of publishing took several years while the intense pleasure of being promoted lasted only several minutes. Within a few days, the joy would completely disappear, as if I never had such success.

Furthermore, I had to remind myself that the race was not over. I had to work even harder to be promoted to full professorship. The university at which I was working had relatively high standards for such a promotion. I had to publish in top ranking journals to earn my promotion.

Pain and pleasure of my career peak

It took another five years to complete the final stage of my academic race. After publishing several strong articles and going through a tough promotion review process, I received the good news. I was promoted to full professorship.

The news was not a big joy at all. I was just relieved that the race was finally over. Strangely, my friends were happier than I was. I did not even mention the promotion to my kids. One day a friend of mine wanted to visit us with his family. We welcomed them. They had a surprise for us. They had made a special cake with the following message: "Congratulations Prof." After they left, my young daughter came to me with a puzzling question: "Daddy, why is your friend congratulating?" I had to tell her that I was just promoted to the full professorship. Obviously, it meant nothing to her since she was not brainwashed yet by the self-deceptive career titles.

I did not remove my previous title from my office door for several months after my promotion. Rather than going around and boosting my ego, I openly confessed to anyone who asked that the title meant absolutely nothing. Indeed, getting to the end was a turning point for me. It was a wake-up call that pursuing position and titles for higher happiness are nothing but self-deception. It could not bring lasting life satisfaction. Here I was at the peak of my career, getting all the titles I had dreamed of. I had an excellent paying job with a net salary that was way above the average salary at the international level. I was relatively well recognized within my specialized field. However, I could not claim that I achieved lasting happiness due to my success. On the contrary, I felt as if I had wasted my life pursuing the wrong things for ultimate dissatisfaction.

Conclusion

I had great hope that my journey of seeking satisfaction through being something would be different. I thought that once I achieved my career dream, I would reach perfect life satisfaction. Once again, I was wrong. After a long and successful journey, I hit the same DEAD loop:

I began my journey as a Mr. Nobody. I was thirsty for respect and recognition. I had no attention from anyone other than my own parents. It was a great pleasure to get close to any respected person. Indeed, I competed to pour water on the hands of respected, wealthy people in the village. My deprivation of respect became the driving force to follow a long, but very successful career. From being a lonely shepherd who was not even respected by the villagers, I managed to gain a certain degree of national and international recognition through my

Figure 2. DEAD Loop of Happiness with Being

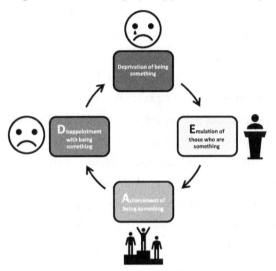

work as a radio and TV host, author of several books, and a full professor with two doctoral degrees. While many people who knew my story expected that I would write a book to tell my success story, hereby, I would like to confess that my journey of seeking life satisfaction through having, doing, and being ended with ultimate failure in finding lasting happiness.

The pursuit of recognition did not bring satisfaction for several reasons. First, like possessions (having) and experiences (doing), positions (beings) are also subject to diminishing marginal utility. In the beginning, the positive feeling of gaining any position is very short lived. It is just a matter of days if not hours to get to zero. On the other hand, the pain of earning a position is much higher. Sometimes, it takes months to score a success point while it takes only minutes to lose the associated joy.

Second, as predicted by the adaptation principle, it does not matter how greatly we succeed, it is just a matter of time until we adapt to the new position and engage in upward comparison.

Third, as well-documented by many empirical studies, the upward comparison is detrimental to subjective well-being. When it comes to a career, it is hard not to engage in such a comparison.

Fourth, as revealed by materialism studies, pursuing possession as extrinsic aspiration is likely to decrease subjective well-being. Indeed, it is a form of slavery, enslaving individuals to the praise of others.

Fifth, seeking a higher position is likely to feed egoistic character, which is detrimental to inner peace and happiness. Indeed, in my opinion, egoism is a form of racism. I believe in perfect equality in terms of innate human value. Thus, in my judgment, we should neither see anyone above ourselves nor see ourselves above anyone in terms of the intrinsic value of being a human being. Claiming to be superior to others as a human due to factors such as race, wealth, gender, or position is a form of racism. I tend to agree with Schopenhauer[4] that the suffering in life is due to our egoistic will. He argues that we are being punished for our nasty egoistic will. In my experience, ego-boosting accomplishment can increase only our suffering, not our genuine satisfaction.

Finally, career success is likely to make us forget our shortcomings and our vulnerable nature as a human being. It blinds us to the waiting reality of eventually being dependent again and being mortal.

As seen in Figure 3, pursuing recognition through being something does shift the marginal utility curve to the right. As a result, the combined marginal utility is higher than that of having and doing. However, we are still seeking happiness in one dimension. Thus, we face the same reality of diminishing marginal utility. We can move along the same dimension only by going backward and forward. As our marginal utility falls, we can climb back to the higher utility by seeking happiness in different things. However, we cannot reverse the law of diminishing utility. Therefore, we will eventually hit the bottom.

In short, as we realize that our utility from having, doing, and being is doomed to approach zero over time, our life satisfaction will also approach zero. In other words, our marginal happiness function of H_{h3} = U (Having, Doing, Being) is going to approach to zero over time:

$$\Delta H_{h3} \rightarrow 0 \text{ as } \Delta U \rightarrow 0$$

---

4   See, Schopenhauer, A. *The Essays of Arthur Schopenhauer: On Human Nature*. T. B. Saunders (tr.). 1860. Reprinted in The Project Gutenberg EBook of The Essays of Arthur Schopenhauer, 2004.

Figure 3. Long-term Marginal Utility of Being Something (reputation and fame)

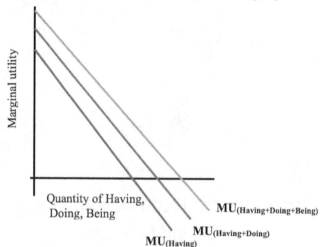

Assuming no afterlife, our total utility based on having, doing, and being will also become zero with death, which has an increasing probability as we age. Thus, we will be desperate to move to another dimension in our search for happiness; else, we will sink into depression. As Charles Taylor (2007, 356) discusses in his famous book, *A Secular Age*, "Modern identity and outlook flattens the world, leaves no place for the spiritual, the higher, for mystery." The highest we can go is the second dimension. It is very hard to transcend beyond that. That is why many people in developed countries feel a terrible sense of flatness in their lives. They sense the emptiness in repeated cycles of desire to consume and disappointment in the result.

Chapter 5

Searching for Hedonic Happiness through Loving

"Love rests on no foundation. It is an endless ocean, with no beginning or end."
—Rumi

Introduction

Indeed, Rumi was right. We have a capacity for infinite love. We never come across someone who runs out of love, and therefore, can't love anymore. Of course, that does not mean we love everything in life. We look for some reasons to give our love. Generally speaking, we love something which seems beautiful, excellent, pleasant, or beneficial. Though we might disagree on what constitutes those qualities, we would agree that we need to have at least one of them to direct our love to someone or something. Likewise, we also agree it is necessary to have love for a happy life. However, that does not mean that falling in love always leads to happiness. In fact, most of the love stories end up with misery. In this chapter, we will add loving (L) to the hedonic happiness equation as a fourth element:

H$_{h4}$ = U (Having, Doing, Being, Loving)

Love is the essence of all life experiences. Love is embedded into having, doing, and being. Love is also the attachment we establish with other humans. Indeed, it is hard to imagine life without love. It is like gravity, holding everything together. We would be dispersed into space if gravity ceased to exist. Likewise, it is not possible to live together if we have no love. In the happiness equation above, loving as a distinct variable refers to our relationship with others. That comes in two forms: friendship and romantic love. Both are extremely important in our search for happiness. The better and deeper relationship leads to higher and lasting happiness. On the other hand, it is love that causes great pain because of rejection or detachment.

Given the potential great pleasure from love, it is hard to imagine hedonic happiness without love. It is necessary to go beyond having, doing, and being to reach the peak of happiness as shown below:

Figure 1. Hedonic Happiness with Having, Doing, Being, and Loving

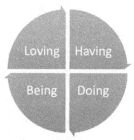

Four Noble Truths on Pain and Pleasure in Love

Buddha famously claimed that we all have to accept the following four truths in pursuing pleasure in life:

1. Life is not possible without suffering (the Truth of Suffering)
2. Suffering is caused by desire and attachment (the Source of Suffering)
3. Desire and attachment can be overcome (the Truth of Cessation)

4. The way to overcome desire and attachment is by the enlightened path (the Truth of the Path).

From this perspective, desire and attachment resulting from love is the source of suffering. That is because whenever we love something, we become attached to it. This attachment gives pleasure. However, whenever we become detached, we experience pain. According to Buddha, the pain of detachment is far higher than the pleasure of attachment. Therefore, we shall cease our desire and attachment. In other words, we shall stop loving anything or anyone. That is not easy, if even possible. We suggest ending the pain of detachment through moving to higher dimensions.

Love in Three Dimensions

What we want to accomplish through both friendship and romantic love depends on the dimension in which we pursue happiness. At the hedonic dimension, we love someone for the expected pleasure from the relationship. In reality, this is not a genuine love for the person we consider a friend or partner. It is the love of the pleasure-seeking self. Therefore, it will cease as soon as we stop receiving pleasure/benefit from that relationship.

The romantic love at the hedonic dimension is mainly for the sake of sexual pleasure. However, the law of diminishing marginal utility will eventually destroy that relationship. Sooner or later, it will come to an end. The hedonist will begin searching for another love, though the end result will always be the same.

At the eudemonic dimension, we aim for a meaningful outcome from love. We establish a friendship with others for a common cause. For instance, we can build a good friendship with someone in working on some meaningful projects. The attachment is the shared goals. The friendship will last as long as the shared goals are alive. Romantic love is for the sake of establishing a family and raising children. We will endure challenges throughout the marriage as long as we believe in the importance of family and raising children as a higher purpose in life. However, if we cease to see the expected meaningful gains to be greater than the pains, we will have difficulty in maintaining the relationship.

At the G-donic dimension, we consider God as the ultimate object of love while everything else would be just a means to the love of God. The friendship, as well as marriage, is for the sake of God. For those who reach the highest level of the G-donic dimension, God is the only one worthy of infinite love because He is the only One with infinite beauty, infinite perfection, infinite kindness, and infinite compassion. Just as beautiful colors of all objects are in reality the beauty of the sun because they are just the reflection of the sunlight, whatever we find worthy of love in life is nothing but the manifestation of God's attributes. Thus, for believers, sincere love shall be only for God. Everything else shall be loved in the name of God.

At the G-donic dimension, when you establish your friendship for the sake of God, you consider your friendship to be eternal. Good attributes of a good friend are just the manifested attributes of God. You love them as the reflection of God's attributes. Of course, that does not mean you should love everything coming from your friends. You should direct your dislike toward bad behaviors or attributes, not the person. You shall help your friends to make positive changes. Whatever you do for your friends shall be only for the sake of God. That means you shall not expect anything in return. You shall expect your reward from God alone. It is hard to be disappointed as long as you do everything for the sake of God with zero expectation from your friends. With such an attitude, you will establish a good relationship with almost everyone.

At the G-donic dimension, love for your partner is also for the sake of God. You will consider your partner as an eternal soulmate created by God. You will establish your relationship based not on transient beauty and benefit, but on eternal ones. For instance, you will love the beauty of your wife as the manifested beauty of God. Even if she losses her beauty as she ages, you believe that she will gain her it back in the hereafter. Furthermore, you will not limit your love to physical beauty alone. Rather, you will direct your love toward the beauty of her soul, which could get better as she gains more wisdom through aging.

Deprivation and Emulation Phase of Searching for Happiness through Loving

Like most everyone, it did not take a long time for me to think that finding love would bring ultimate happiness. Unlike many, I was raised in a society in which love was completely taboo. I was not supposed to fall in love before marriage. Love was not a goal. It was just a gift for establishing a family. In other words, love at the hedonic dimension was not allowed. Therefore, my love experience falls into the eudemonic and G-donic dimensions. However, I had many opportunities to observe those who went through hedonic love. Thus, I will rely largely on personal observation when talking about that form of love.

Though explicit love was forbidden in our village, it was not dead. The fountain in the middle of the village was an excellent opportunity for young men and women to court each other. As it was a culturally conservative society, there was no public domain for mingling. Girls were not supposed to talk to strangers. They would lose their chance of getting married if there was even a suspicion that they were flirting. The secret lovers had to make sure that they ran into each other on the way to the fountain by pure luck. Instead of the public camera, they were being monitored by the public view. Someone was always watching.

Many would wait for marriage in order to experience love. That is why marriage was the most important life event to look forward. The wedding ceremonies would take days. I remember we used to gather at the groom's house in the night for almost forty days to play a wedding. For young bachelors like me, the marriage would be the pinnacle of happiness. Sometimes, I would imagine how my future wife would look like or where she was now. Of course, I had no idea about that.

Indeed, in the village, most of the marriages were arranged. Given that it was a patriarchal society, the marriage decision would be made by the groom's side. It was the groom's parents who would pick a bride. Mostly, it would be the mom's choice. The bride would be chosen based on her skills to help the mom. The love relationship was not a factor. It was assumed to be there after the marriage. Actually, I remember several weddings in which the groom and bride would see each other for the first time at the wedding night. That was the case particularly when the bride came from another village.

Ironically, despite the weird arranged marriages, divorce was almost unheard of. Even if the couples later learned that they were not a good match, they would sustain their marriage for the sake of children.

Accomplishment and Disappointment Phase of Searching for Happiness through Loving

After I left the village, I managed to break some taboos. My marriage was not arranged by my parents. Instead, a friend of mine who got married before me helped me to find a candidate. After gathering some information about her, I met my future wife a few times before making a final decision. We both explored each other's expectations to make sure that we had shared goals and matching characters. We arranged our wedding ceremony right after the very last exam before my graduation from college. I remember that I had to run right after the exam to catch the ceremony. It has been 25 years since that ceremony. We are still married with six children.

I shall confess that the early days of emotional love are long gone. However, that does not mean we do not have a happy marriage. Of course, there have been ups and downs. The fact that we made our 25th anniversary is a clear testimony to our successful relationship. I am not sure we could have made it if we were pursuing hedonic happiness.

Indeed, there is considerable evidence that hedonic happiness and marriage are not compatible with each other. Given the fact that hedonism is now dominant at the global level, it is not surprising to see that family institutions are being shattered. As presented in Chapter 11, more and more people opt not to get married at all. Among those who are married, half of them end up with a divorce. On the other hand, dating and having multiple sexual partners throughout life are becoming the norm while marriages are becoming rare.

Perhaps, it is the first time in history that we have eliminated all religious and cultural barriers standing in front of all kinds of love affairs. Since the 1960s, we have seen a sexual revolution that made free love a popular term. Particularly, with birth control, legal abortion, and women's liberation, we eliminated all barriers to free love. However, it is hard to claim that having multiple sexual partners would make you better off than sticking with one partner through a marital contract. In fact, many scientific studies in the last two decades clearly revealed that married people are happier than unmarried ones. Furthermore, the subjective wellbeing data also show that we are not happier than in the 1960s.

We argue that the loving affairs at the hedonic dimension are subject to the DEAD loop as shown in Figure 2 below. As we are deprived of romantic love, we envy those who are successful in finding loving partners. However, as we accomplish our goal, the honeymoon period will be short-lived. We generally begin with a promise for permanent love. We think that we find a true soul mate. In the beginning, love blinds us to see any shortcoming in our partner. As time passes, our love will fade away. We will become blind to even good sides of our partner. That is when we will look for an excuse to break up with great pain and disappointment.

Figure 2. DEAD Loop of Happiness with Loving

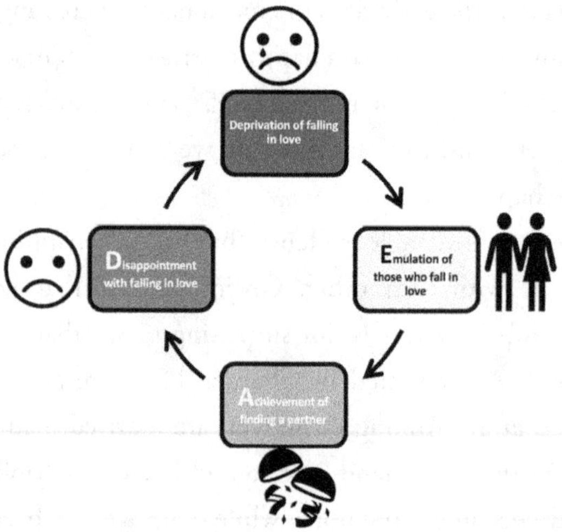

Conclusion

We begin our happiness journey as an adult, thinking that love is a way to reach the peak of happiness. When we first fall in love, we promise that it will last forever. In fact, when we are in love, we are committed to someone, so it feels like she/he is the only one for us. As if we are meant to be. However, if it is a hedonic love, for sure, it might not last even for a year. That is because of the law of diminishing marginal utility (pleasure). Sooner or later, we will get tired of our partner and break up to search for another one. For most people, the detachment will really hurt.

I never forget an incident I observed when I was at a hospital doing my internship to be a nurse. A young man who was in his early twenties came to the emergency department with some severe injuries to his both arms. While treating his injuries, I asked him how he got injured. He said he did it to himself. I was shocked to hear that. I asked him why he did it. He said it was because of the breakup with his girlfriend. Years later, when I read Buddha, I remembered that incident as a confirming case of potential pain from love. It was clear that the pain of detachment was far above the pain of self-injury for that young man. You do not have to be an expert to know the degree of disappointment among lovers. Just pay attention to songs, movies, and novels; most of them are loud cries from the painful experience of lovers.

Can we experience love without great pain? More importantly, can we love someone forever? Theoretically speaking, yes. However, not at the hedonic dimension.

Chapter 6

Scientific Research of Hedonic Happiness

"A cynic is a man who knows the price of everything and the value of nothing."

—Oscar Wilde

Introduction

Happiness is one of the topics most explored by various experts, including philosophers, theologians, psychologists, and economists. In essence, they all try to discover some guiding principles for a happy life. The doctrine of hedonism in terms of maximizing pleasure and minimizing pain was first suggested in ancient times. Some thinkers such as Epicurus (342–270 BCE) argued that it is our moral obligation to pursue maximum pleasure in life. While many religious figures denounced hedonism as a path to a sinful life, some Renaissance philosophers such as Erasmus (1466–1536) and Thomas Moore (1478–1535) argued that it was God's wish that we pursue happiness.

In economics, Jeremy Bentham (1748–1832) was the first one using hedonism to lay the foundation for utilitarianism. Despite some objections, happiness is still alive in economics. We even have a subfield called economics of happiness. Likewise, in modern psychology, the growing field of positive psychology explores many dimensions of happiness, while hedonic psychology as a subfield deals with the hedonic dimension of happiness.

Hedonism and Consumer Culture

In a modern consumer society, individuals put great importance on materialistic goals to achieve higher happiness. Indeed, one might argue that the quest for happiness is pursued mainly through material consumption. From a utilitarian hedonic perspective, the more one consumes, the happier one will be. It is vital for people to make more money and have more possessions (Aydin 2012). They do not consume goods and services solely for functional needs, but rather use them as a symbol to communicate personal, social, and cultural messages to others (McCracken 1988). Indeed, consumers are in a constant process of reconstructing their identity through material consumption. They buy not only products but also prestige, visions, dreams, associations, status, etc.(Klein 2001).

Studies indicate that the new generation is even more hedonic. For instance, an extensive study (Twenge, Campbell, and Freeman 2012) explored the importance of different generations of various types of life goals. The study revealed that younger generations, especially the millennials who were born after 1982, viewed "money, fame, and image" as being among the more important life goals. That study also revealed that younger generations are more likely than older generations to embrace materialist values due to the influence of mass media. Indeed, from a very early age, people are bombarded with messages about the importance of pursuing money, fame, and success for happiness (Dittmar and Halliwell 2008).

Ironically, conspicuous consumer culture is neither sustainable nor desirable for higher happiness. Indeed, a report by the British Royal Society (2012) pointed to the global consumer culture as a significant threat to the planet. The study highlights the dangers for both people and the planet if the current consumer culture is not stopped soon (Royal Society, 2012). The report warned that "Rapid and widespread changes in the world's human population, coupled with unprecedented levels of consumption present profound challenges to human health and wellbeing, and the natural environment." Twenty-two scientists who contributed to the report offered nine recommendations to prevent "social, economic and environmental failures and catastrophes on a scale never imagined" within 30-40 years. They explicitly called for a reduction of material consumption and for the development of socio-economic systems and institutions that are not dependent on continued material consumption growth.

Intrinsic and Extrinsic Aspirations

Researchers divide life goals into two main categories: intrinsic and extrinsic (Kasser and Ryan, 1996). Intrinsic goals are driven mostly by essential human needs whereas extrinsic goals focus on seeking approval/appreciation from others. Intrinsic motivations are driven by a certain element within oneself; extrinsic motivations are driven by external elements, such as social pressure or feelings of guilt. Intrinsic goals are linked to the fulfillment of psychological needs for relatedness, autonomy, and competence as suggested by self-determination theory.

In contrast, extrinsic goals are driven by external reward or social praise. In other words, extrinsic motivation appeals to others whereas intrinsic motivation appeals to one's inner elements. Researchers measure extrinsic and intrinsic goals through the Aspiration Index (AI). Many empirical studies clearly show that extrinsic aspirations are negatively correlated to happiness.

Money, Materialism, and Happiness

Extrinsic aspirations are mostly materialistic, meaning they place great importance on money as a means to success and happiness. Research in consumer behavior has found that materialist people perceive consumption as a way to build and portray themselves to others (Eastman, Goldsmith, and Flynn 1999). Their consumer motivations and brand engagement are intertwined with each other in self-concept (Sprott, Czellar, and Spangenberg 2009). Eastman et al. (1999) demonstrated that among American college students, materialism in the form of possessing goods is strongly linked to seeking social status. Heaney et al. (2005) confirmed the same findings among Malaysian students.

Since the mid-1980s, many studies have revealed that materialist aspirations are negatively associated with subjective wellbeing (SWB). The more importance people give to materialist goals, such as making more money and having more possessions, the less happiness, life satisfaction, and self-actualization they achieve (Richins and Dawson 1992). Furthermore, the more materialistic they are, the higher they score on anxiety, depression, and other psychological problems (Kasser 2002). These findings have been confirmed across different demographic groups, including children (Banerjee and Dittmar 2008), college students (Niemiec, Ryan, and Deci 2009), and adults (Burroughs and Rindfleisch 2002). Indeed, a recent meta-analysis of many studies conducted in the last two decades revealed strong evidence regarding the negative association between materialist aspirations and SWB (Aydin and Manusov 2014; Dittmar et al. 2014).

Some consumer researchers have also confirmed these findings (Richins and Dawson 1992). They revealed that, compared to those with low levels of materialism, those with high levels of materialism have an underlying feeling of insecurity, poor interpersonal relationships, and a low or contingent sense of self-esteem. Also, those with a high level of materialism tend to ignore psychological need-satisfying behaviors, such as social engagement and affiliation (B et al. 2006).

Money can buy happiness only if you are poor

Many studies have investigated the relationship between household income and SWB (Bettingen and Luedicke, 2009; Xiao and Kim, 2009; Zhong and Mitchell, 2010). The findings have been mixed. It seems that money does matter for those who do not have enough. However, it does not matter once an individual exceeds a certain income threshold. As long as money serves to fulfill basic needs, it makes a difference (Cummins, Gullone, and Lau 2002; Witt 2010). Once basic needs are met, additional income makes marginal or no contribution to SWB.

In his pioneering work, Easterlin (1974) demonstrated that in the United States, average SWB remained stagnant from 1946 through 1970 despite tremendous economic growth during that period. Easterlin subsequently conducted a similar study for Japan and found that the average self-reported happiness level did not increase in Japan between 1958 and 1987 despite a fivefold increase in real income. Since then, many studies have confirmed that more wealth and more consumption do not necessarily increase human happiness.

In fact, some studies have even found a negative relationship between higher consumption and SWB (Ahuvia 2008). One study has suggested that higher income could reduce dissatisfaction, but not increase satisfaction (Boes and Winkelmann 2010). In other words, money could help reduce pain, but not bring more pleasure, which is contrary to what many might think.

In a study (Aydin 2017) of nearly 900 randomly selected individuals in Istanbul, we explored the role of money in buying happiness. Our study confirmed the positive relationship between income and subjective well-being. However, it showed that if you are money-minded, you are less satisfied. Furthermore, when we divided the sample into two groups based on their income in respect to the median income of the entire sample, the regression result revealed that the low-income earners had relatively higher life satisfaction. Thus, we concluded that money is important for the poor, but not really helpful for the rich. In other words, you can buy happiness with money only if you are among the poor.

Seeking Lost Self-Worth through Luxury Consumption[5]

We buy goods and services not just for their functions, but also for their psychological effects. That is why in economics we put goods and services into two categories: functional and positional. Of course, some might fall in both categories. Particularly, luxury products provide esteem and prestige to consumers in addition to their functional utilities (Arghavan and Zaichkowsky, 2000). The functional utility of luxury products might even exceed their positional utility (Vigneron and Johnson, 2004). Relatively speaking, we can define luxury products as those "whose ratio of functional utility to price is low while the ratio of intangible and situational utility to price is high" (Nueno and Quelch, 1998). Thus, conspicuous consumption means buying luxury goods and services to show off one's economic power as a means of either attaining or maintaining a

---

5   For further information, please refer to my following published article: "Seeking Self-Worth Through Commodity Narcissism & Commodity Nihilism in the Light of Secular and Tawhidi Paradigms", Al-Shajarah: Journal of the International Institute of Islamic Thought & Civilization, Volume: 18, Issue: 2 Pages: 175-201.

certain social status. The concept was first used by Thorstein Veblen (1857-1929) in his book, *The Theory of the Leisure Class* to describe the luxury consumption of the rich social class that was the product of the Industrial Revolution.

Luxury consumption is as old as human history. Luxury products have always been highly esteemed by people. With the depiction of the Western lifestyle in various media outlets at the global level, the desire for conspicuous consumption has reached an all-time high. This is even the case for consumers in emerging markets. With the media portraying a luxury lifestyle as an elegant means to happiness, an increasing number of people in the world now engage in conspicuous consumption (Shukla, 2011).

Why do people engage in conspicuous consumption? People buy luxury products for many reasons such as product quality, social comparison, social pressure, investment for future, self-actualization, high status, etc. Many studies suggest that luxury consumption is driven by value/status-seeking behavior. In other words, people do not buy high-status goods for their function, but mostly for their position. For that matter, it is essential to explore human value (self-worth) since the Industrial Revolution to understand the intrinsic motivation behind luxury consumption. One can argue that the human has lost his intrinsic worth since the Enlightenment. He tries to regain his value through the value of his possession(Aydin 2013).

Commodity Fetishism and Commodity Narcissism

Post-modern structuralism and semiotics help us to decode value-seeking commodity fetishism. Judith Williamson, in *Decoding Advertisement* (1978), explains how advertisers convey such false messages to consumers. For instance, a cigarette advertisement with the image of a cowboy on horseback associates power, health, wealth and outdoor activity with smoking. Thus, smokers might think that they will be empowered when they smoke a certain brand of cigarette. Similarly, ads for expensive perfume always use beautiful models pursued by handsome men, suggesting that women who use that perfume will appear more attractive to men.

In *Capital, Volume One*, Marx attempts to define commodity fetishism and its secrets. He argues that in a capitalist society, consumers act as if goods are self-sustained with their qualities and characteristics, mistakenly denying the fact that they come from labor. Consumers thereby mystify objects, assuming they have self-properties while they know in reality that is not true. This is quite similar to the totemic belief in ancient society. Billig argues that commodity fetishism functions "through a process of social forgetting" (Billig, 1999, p.315).

Commodity fetishism also might help to understand conspicuous consumption, with some modification in meaning. Consumers make a fetish of luxury commodities by pretending they can gain specific value. They try to satisfy their innate desire to be a worthy person in the universe by possessing expensive commodities. Even though they know that the quality of commodities could not translate into their human quality, they pretend that it can. They think that the value of their commodities defines their own value.

The other concept which might help to understand conspicuous consumption is "commodity narcissism." Freud came up with this concept. He argues that people pursue narcissistic satisfaction by thinking they are better than others through material possession (Freud, 1962). Commodity narcissism is to elevate oneself over others through luxury consumption. The self-love is contained in the object-love. However, when commodity fetishism is combined with commodity narcissism, consumers will engage in the elevation of themselves to the destruction of others (Cluley and Dunne, 2012). For a narcissist, society is divided into two groups, rich and poor. He tries to distinguish himself from the poor and ordinary by being and looking different through conspicuous consumption.

Luxury Consumption and Subjective Well-Being

The oil-rich Gulf countries have become the hub of luxury consumption through their shopping malls and consumer culture. Riyadh, Dubai, and Qatar are the target cities for the luxury goods market. To see whether luxury consumption brings more happiness in the Gulf Cooperation Council (GCC) countries, we conducted a short survey in 2012 among seventy undergraduate business college students in Riyadh to measure the relationship between luxury consumption and subjective well-being. We aimed to test the hypothesis that luxury consumption would positively correlate to subjective well-being. We picked a car's value as a proxy for luxury consumption and asked randomly selected juniors about their car's value, the pleasure they received while driving to the college on that day, and overall satisfaction with their life.

The first question was about the car's value. We gave them five different price ranges to identify their car's value. Almost half of the students reported owning a vehicle valued above 80,000 Saudi Riyals (SAR) (about $21,330 USD). This means they owned relatively expensive cars. Indeed, for students, any car's above 40,000 SAR ($10,665 USD) could be considered luxury.

The second question was about the enjoyment of driving. We asked the survey participants about their pleasure of driving on that day. While 46% of students received some pleasure from driving, 38% percent received no pleasure. We measured the Pearson correlation coefficient to see whether having an expensive car correlated with higher satisfaction with life. The correlation between the car's value and life satisfaction turned to be less than 0.1, statistically showing almost zero correlation. The correlation coefficient for enjoying driving and the car's value was even less. Both coefficients clearly rejected the hypothesis that there is a positive correlation between the car's value and pleasure from driving or satisfaction in life.

Conclusion

Pursuing wealth and consumption is good only if it fulfills a function helping people to disclose their potential. That is why the evidence regarding the impact of materialist values is somewhat mixed. Although many studies have revealed the importance of income in SWB, others have shown that higher income is not necessarily linked to higher well-being. It seems that the driving motivation behind financial success does matter. If a person perceives money as an important means to satisfy basic psychological needs, it contributes positively to SWB; however, if it is a means to power, fame, or pleasure, it is detrimental to well-being.

PART II

SEEKING HAPPINESS IN MEANING (EUDEMONIC) DIMENSION

Chapter 7

Aristotle's Eudemonic Happiness Model[6]

"Joy is man's passage from a less to a greater perfection"
—Spinoza

Introduction

Who is happy? For the ancient Greeks, it is hard to know the answer. They put meaning at the center of happiness by saying, "Call no man happy until he is dead." In other words, your happiness shall not be measured by what pleasure you receive. Instead, it shall be measured by your accomplishment. Since you have a certain potential, like a seed, you shall be happy only if you unleash your potential and bear fruit.

Means and Ends

Aristotle attempted to provide a practical answer on how to live a happy life. He was one of the first people who tried to answer the happiness question

6   This topic is part of the following paper presented at Harvard University: "Islamic Economics: New Paradigm or Old Capitalism?" was presented at *10th Harvard Forum of Islamic Finance, Harvard University*, March 24-25, 2012, Boston, USA.

systematically. Not counting the Divine scripts, his book *Nicomachean Ethics* was the first written attempt to find an answer to this age-old question. Even though it was the first ethics book teaching how to live a good life, it is still an essential one in its field. Aristotle also examined '*oikonomia*,' which literally means the management of the household, in his book, *Politica*. He used an analogy to understand the mission or function of our life on this planet. He began with an example of a craftsman who works for an end: "Every craft [*technē*] and every line of inquiry [*methodos*], and likewise every action [*praxis*] and decision [*proairesis*], seems to seek some good; that is why some people were right to describe the good as what everything seeks" (Aristotle, 1999, p.1094a 1-5).

According to Aristotle, we all aim for an end (some good things) in our actions and thoughts. Particularly as a rational being, we deliberately choose the means for an end in our lives: "Deliberation is about the actions he can do, and actions are for the sake of other things; hence we deliberate about things that promote an end, not about the end (Aristotle, 1999, p.1112b 32-35). However, there are two types of end outcomes we are aiming for. One is intermediate, and the other is final. We value intermediate ends because of their contribution to the final ends. In other words, anything is good if it serves the final end, which is also called the "final good" or "highest good". Aristotle agreed that there could be multiple goods; however, they could be ordered hierarchically. In other words, some goods are sought not for their own sake, but for something else. For instance, health is good by itself and also because of its role in reaching happiness.

Figure 1. Means and final ends

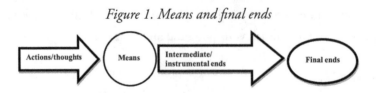

Highest Good: Happiness

For Aristotle, the final or highest good is the end for the sake of which everything else is done. Even though he accepted multiple goods, he argued that there is one final good that everyone seeks. This is happiness (*eudaimonia*). Aristotle provided two reasons for his argument of the final good/end: completeness (final) and self-sufficiency. In other words, everything but happiness is desired for some other reason while happiness is desired for itself. It is complete and sufficient requiring nothing else. The happy person needs nothing more because happiness is self-sufficient: "The 'self-sufficient' we posit as being what in isolation makes life desirable and lacking in nothing, and we think that happiness is like this and moreover most desirable of all things, it not being counted with other goods: clearly, if it *were* so counted in with the least of other goods, we would think it more desirable, for what is added becomes an extra quantity of goods, and the larger amount of goods is always more desirable" (Aristotle, 1999p, 1097b14-21).

Figure 2. Two traits of happiness

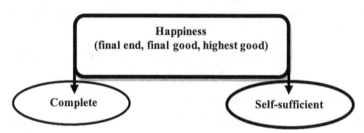

If the highest good is happiness, then, we still need to know what happiness is: "But presumably the remark that the best good is happiness is apparently something [generally] agreed, and we still need a clearer statement of what the best good is. Perhaps, then, we shall find this if we first grasp the function of human beings. For just as the good, i.e. [doing] well, for a flutist, a sculptor, and every craftsman, and, in general, for whatever has a function and [characteristic] action, seems to depend on its function, the same seems to be true for a human being, if a human being has some function" (Aristotle, 1999, p.1097b 23-29). He then raised the question about the kind of life we are supposed to live to reach the highest good. He responded that we should live according to our nature. As a rational being, he argued, the function of our life is "the activity of the soul in accordance with reason, or not apart from reason"(Aristotle, 1999, p.1098a 8). "Each function is completed well by being completed in a way in accord with the virtue (arête) proper to that kind of thing" (Aristotle, 1999, p.1098a 16-18).

Happiness and virtue

Aristotle attempted to define happiness by distinguishing three different traits of the soul: affections, capacities, and dispositions (Aristotle, 1999, p.1105b 20). He argued that happiness is not a pleasure even though it comes with pleasure. Happiness is a virtue. In other words, happiness is to live a virtuous life. For that matter, happiness is not knowledge of what is virtuous. It is living by virtue. Therefore, it is not thought, it is action. Nor is it merely affection and capacity: "We are neither called good nor called bad nor are we praised or blamed, insofar as we are simply capable of feelings. Further, while we have capacities by nature, we do not become good or bad by nature" (Aristotle, 1999, p.1106a 8-12). In Aristotle's terms, happiness "is activity in accord with virtue" (Aristotle, 1999, p.1098b 31).

Capacities and knowledge are not sufficient to be virtues and happiness if they are not translated into actions. A great person who spends all of his time asleep will not be considered virtuous even if he knows and embraces every kind of virtue. "Presumably, though, it matters quite a bit whether we suppose that the best good consists in possessing or in using virtue, that is to say, in a state or in an activity [that actualizes that state]. For someone may be in a state that achieves no good if, for instance, he is asleep or inactive in some other way, but this cannot be true of the activity. For it will necessarily act and act well. And just as Olympic prizes are not for the finest and the strongest, but for the contestants since it is only those who win, the same is true in life; among the fine and good people, only those who act correctly win the prize" (Aristotle, 1999, pp.1098b 32- 1099a 6).

Figure 3. Happiness through virtuous actions

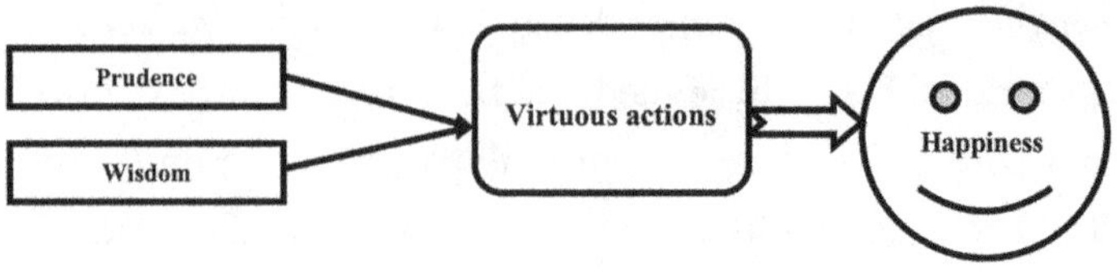

Virtuous life

If happiness is the highest good that can be achieved through virtuous actions, then one needs to know what is virtue and how to be virtuous: "Since happiness is a certain sort of activity in accord with complete virtue, we must examine virtue; for that will perhaps also be a way to study happiness better (Aristotle, 1999, p.1102a 5-8). According to Aristotle, virtue is excellence in life. Excellence is moderation. Excellence can be known through "practical intelligence" or what is called prudence (rationally acquired knowledge about what is good) and wisdom (theoretical knowledge of necessary truths). That is why Aristotle said that "one has all the virtues if and only if one has prudence"(Aristotle, 1999, p.1145a 2). Whoever employs his mind in a proper way will understand that living well is living in moderation. He will assign the appropriate weight to each virtue considering its contribution to the final good: happiness. If the person fails to do so, he will not be considered wise or prudent. In other words, living well is to act wisely in terms of making a choice for the final good. It is to stay away from excessiveness and deficiency. It is striking the mean. It is a balance point between a deficiency and an excess of a trait. For example, courage is the mean between fearfulness and foolhardiness, confidence is the mean between self-deprecation and arrogance, and generosity is the mean between stinginess and wastefulness.

Happiness = Virtuous life = Excellence/moderation

Knowing what is good is not sufficient to be good or to have a good life. In Aristotle's view, actions in line with virtue are necessary for a happy life. Then, the question is whether one needs to have external means to accomplish a happy life. Even though according to Aristotle, happiness is a merit for the human soul, rather than the body, it is still important to have the means to be happy: "It is impossible or not easy to perform fine actions if one is without resources" (Aristotle, 1999, p.1099a 33). He did not necessarily mean wealth or consumer goods. He meant education and moral training to learn about virtue and moderation as a way to a happy life. For that matter, eudemonia means human flourishing more than a pleasant experience that is associated with happiness. In Aristotle's writings, human excellence is embedded with a pleasant feeling. They are not separable.

Three types of pleasure

Aristotle did not value a life pursuit of sensual or egotistic pleasures. In his view, people generally pursue three kinds of pleasures in their lives: sensual, egoistic (or pleasure of honor) and intellectual (contemplative) pleasures. The first type is unique to the animal while the second one is common among politicians. However, the third one, which is the highest and most worthy one, is unique to human beings. Even though Aristotle considered the highest pleasure to come from a contemplative/virtuous life, he did not think that pleasure was the highest goal. In other words, his happiness model is not hedonic; it is eudemonic. Indeed, he argued that bad pleasures could even lead to an unhappy life: "Most people are deceived, and the deception seems to come about because of pleasure; for it appears a good thing when it is not. So, they choose what is pleasant as something good, and they avoid pain as something bad" (Aristotle, 1999, p.1113a 35-b2). Aristotle is not against good pleasure: "The pleasure belonging to a worthwhile activity is good, while that related to a worthless one is bad; for appetites, too, are praiseworthy when they are for fine things, and worthy of censure when they are for shameful things" (Aristotle, 1999, p.1175b 25). Therefore, it is important to use practical wisdom to identify "bad/misleading pleasures." It is essential to pursue pleasure in virtuous actions, not in vice.

Conclusion

For Aristotle, happiness is the highest good because it is complete and self-sufficient. In his understanding, practical reason clearly indicates that the ultimate purpose of human life is to act in a rational manner. That rationality would lead us to moderation in living a good life. There are two crucial problems with such reasoning. First, Aristotle perceived the human mind as the sole source of virtue. In reality, the human mind could fail to determine virtue. In other words, what society thinks of as virtue might not be real virtue. Second, if life is limited to this world, it would be hard to justify lasting virtuous actions. Since everything will eventually be annihilated, the ultimate result of human endeavors will be nothing as confessed by Bernard Russell: "all the labors of the ages, all the devotion, all the inspiration, all the noonday brightness of human genius, are destined to extinction in the vast death of the solar system." The human mind does not see any goodness in making an effort for nothing. Gaining excellence to decay in the grave is not satisfactory.

In short, in the eudemonic model, happiness is the byproduct of an accomplished life. You are happy when you are fully immersed in certain activities that unleash your potential. In Taylor's terms, "Somewhere, in some activity, or condition, lies a fullness, a richness; that is, in that place (activity or condition), life is fuller, richer, deeper, more worthwhile, more admirable, more what it should be." (Taylor, 2007, introduction, section 2).

Chapter 8

Searching for Eudemonic Happiness through Meaning

"What is this life? A frenzy, an illusion a shadow, a delirium, a fiction. The greatest good's but little, and this life is but a dream, and dreams are only dreams."

—Pedro Calderón de la Barca

Introduction

My search for happiness through maximizing hedonic utility by having, doing, and being ended with disappointment. I felt that I was stuck in a DEAD hedonic loop of Deprivation, Emulation, Achievement, and Disappointment. Luckily, I have learned through personal experience and reading of scientific findings that happiness is possible through a flourishing and meaningful life. That is known as eudemonic happiness as discussed in the previous chapter. The objective is to maximize virtue through meaningful accomplishments. In my understanding, there are two types of meaning: temporal and transcendental. The former is about seeking meaning in this world while the latter is about exploring meaning beyond this life. In this chapter, we will focus on temporal meaning. We will cover transcendental meaning in the last chapter.

Defining the Meaning of Life

What is the meaning of life? Not sure? Do not feel bad. For thousands of years, we have been seeking a unified answer. The search is not over. Even if we do not have a conclusive answer, we cannot stop asking the same question, again and again, particularly, when we are disappointed with our life. The Oxford English Dictionary (OED) defines "meaning" as "The significance, purpose, underlying truth, etc., of something." Meaning can also be defined as "signification; intention; cause, purpose; motive, justification," … "[o]f an action, condition, etc." Particularly, for human beings, meaning refers to "Something which gives one a sense of purpose, value, etc., esp. of a metaphysical or spiritual kind; the (perceived) purpose of existence or of a person's life. Freq. in the meaning of life." (All this is from the OED.)

Thus, linguistically speaking, meaning is often conceived of as something non-obvious and even secretive that can be decoded by a conscious being. In this sense, seeking the meaning of life is to consider life as a story, puzzle, word, or sign with some deep inner essence that we attempt to discover. Of course, searching for it does not mean that we will find something. That's why Shakespeare's Macbeth characterizes life as, "a tale told by an idiot, full of sound and fury, signifying nothing."

Ancient philosophers such as Socrates argued that it is not worth living if we do not examine life to define its meaning. Many thinkers have explored the meaning of life. Some have concluded that the question of meaning itself is meaningless while others try to come up with an answer. For instance, Schopenhauer argued that the meaning of life is the will to live. However, he said that life is not worth living in terms of following one's own will. Instead, one should deny the self or the will by giving up pursuing desires. Sartre embraced the view that life is meaningless but urged us nonetheless to make a free choice that would give our lives meaning and responsibility. Of course, Sartre's solution contradicts itself, so it is meaningless!

Camus also thought that life is absurd and meaningless. He argued that we are no different from the mythical Greek of old, Sisyphus. We are condemned to pushing a rock up a hill, over and over, only to see it roll back every time we get it to the top of the hill. Like Sisyphus, our effort to find happiness is a pointless cycle of hope and misery.

Kierkegaard found no meaning in anything other than passionate obedience to God. Nietzsche defined the meaning of life as the will to power. He urged people to follow his ideal man (the Übermensch) rather than pursue little pleasure. Bertrand Russell held that a meaningful life is possible only if one cultivates an interest in the eternal. Tolstoy agreed. He suggested that we should naively follow faith to avoid the ultimate meaninglessness of death. For Heidegger, the meaning of life is to read the disclosing meaning of beings.

I was not the first one to recognize the importance of meaning for happiness. Perhaps, the very first scholarly writing on this matter came over two thousand years ago, from Aristotle. As discussed in the previous chapter, in his book, *Nicomachean Ethics*, Aristotle put everything we pursue in life within two categories: means and end. He encouraged us to reflect on the end while pursuing any means. For him, meaningful life is when we pursue a good end through moderation and flourishing. In modern times, we call this type of pursuit of happiness eudemonic happiness. From this perspective, it is not possible to reach authentic happiness through the utility maximization of having, doing, and being without living a meaningful and flourished life. As shown below, the meaning is an additive term to the happiness equation. Eudemonic happiness (He) will be possible if we pursue moderation in utility (U) / pleasure while we try to maximize meaning (M) in having (H), doing (D), being (B), and loving (L):

$$H_{e1} = U\,(H, D, B, L) + M\,(H, D, B, L)$$

I affirm eudemonic happiness through my personal experience. As discussed earlier, I did not find authentic happiness in a hedonic path, although I was very successful in reaching a peak of having, doing, and being. As I added meaning to my life experience through activities such a marriage as discussed in Chapter 5, I would achieve greater satisfaction. For me, living a meaningful life is to bear fruit for oneself and others. In other words, the meaning is the significance in the eyes of conscious beings. Thus, a meaningful life is one with a significant outcome. For instance, saving a stone from a flood and placing it in an elegant palace does not mean anything to that stone. Unless this act of saving the stone means something to someone, we do not consider this act to be meaningful. On the other hand, saving a human being from a flooding river is extremely significant to that person. It is significant to the saver as well, as long as he cares about human life. Planting a stone and watering it is meaningless. However, planting a seed is meaningful because of its expected fruit for living beings.

Two things are real boosters for meaning in terms of producing a significant outcome. One is the value to those we care about. The more we help them through our acts, the more we will be satisfied. As Steve Jobs once said, it is more meaningful and satisfactory to produce amazing devices rather than to sell a sugary drink such as Coca Cola. Even though one might get a higher profit in the Coca Cola business, one would derive higher satisfaction in the high-tech business. That is because of the significance of devices to human beings. The second important determinant of meaning is the duration. The longer the outcome lasts, the more we would find it to be meaningful. Indeed, as Heidegger argued, we do not find any meaning if we do not have any future. The value of the present time includes its impact on the future. Imagine that we reach our highest achievement and receive the highest award such as a Nobel Prize. If we know for sure that the award requires extremely hard work that will cost us our life, we will think it is meaningless to work for such an award. Indeed, Tolstoy depicts such meaningless efforts through the elegant story of a greedy villager who meticulously ran after possessions. As he was about to achieve his goal of being rich, he became exhausted and died.

I argue that as we set goals to make a meaningful contribution by using our potential, we feel higher joy and satisfaction as a byproduct of living a flourishing life. Thus, the search for happiness must include an optimum combination of meaning and utility from having, doing, being, and loving. In other words, hedonic happiness is a unidimensional seeking satisfaction through utility from having, doing, and being. As shown in the graph below, meaning requires adding a new dimension to utility in seeking happiness:

Figure 1. Eudemonic Happiness Dimensions with
Having, Doing, Being, Loving, Meaning

Indeed, as Nietzsche argued, we can endure any suffering as long as it is meaningful. In other words, the real pain lies in a meaningless event because we are a purpose-driven creature. We cannot help asking "why" questions to explore meaning. We can accept pain if the end justifies the means. Unlike in hedonic happiness, we do not need to minimize the pain for maximum happiness. We are fine with having greater pain for greater gain of meaningful outcomes.

In the following sections, through my personal experience and scientific findings, I would like to show the importance of temporal meaning in attaining higher life satisfaction. I will start with my stories of deprived meaning and emulation before telling how I successfully integrated meaning into my overall life and daily events.

Deprivation and Emulation Phase

Like everyone else, my life began with no purpose beyond the instinct to sustain my biological life and have fun. I was not alone. For almost everyone in the village, life had a simple expectation. You were expected to learn how to take care of livestock and do simple farming. Once you reached the age of 20, you would marry to establish family life. That was easy, too. You would live with extended family members while learning how to build a family life and raise children. It was a boring life cycle with no surprises. It was like watching the same movie, again and again. At a very early age, I had the feeling that I would live a life bigger than that of the villagers. I did not want to stay in the village and be a full-time shepherd. For me, education was the only means to escape from village life to find a more meaningful one.

Seeking the meaning of life

For me, meaning always meant aiming for something beyond the means I was currently pursuing. For instance, in elementary school, getting a good grade was a means for me to convince my parents to continue my education further because that would mean escaping from village life. In middle school, I set a goal of passing a competitive exam to go to high school. I knew that my parents could not afford to send me to high school if I did not get a scholarship. Likewise, in high school, I was obsessed with the college entry exam to go to college. At each stage, I would emulate the successful figures that I knew and work hard to be like them. My search for meaning was mostly through trial and error rather than coaching and teaching. I knew that through strong educational degrees, I would have a better life. However, I did not have any specific direction until the end of my college years. My parents were not in a position to guide me beyond elementary school. I had no one else I could trust to give me guidance. Teachers and peers were the main compasses for me. At an early age, I considered teachers as the perfect guide. Soon, I came across different teachers and lost my trust in them. Likewise, it was a great help to have good friends for guidance. However, most of them were as confused as I was.

Suffering in meaningless courses

I have many examples of painful experiences due to the lack of meaning. When I enrolled in middle school, I had to choose a foreign language. I had no idea of the importance of learning a foreign language. I was struggling to learn my second language. It was a torture for me to learn a third language at that time. Since I did not have any preference, I was assigned to a French class. I began learning some French. Soon, I heard from other students that the French would not help me in my future career. I had no choice of changing to English. From then onward, I saw no meaning in learning French beyond getting a grade. I had to live with this pain until I went to college. Each time, I would study well for the exam and get a very high grade. Then, I would forget everything. Despite several years of studying French, I now barely remember a few words in French. This has nothing to do with my foreign language skills. Around the age of forty, I began studying Arabic because I was convinced that it was necessary for me since I had moved to live in Saudi Arabia. Within a year, I began communicating with people in Arabic without any problem.

It was not easy to find self-direction in the pre-internet era. I remember how confused I was while trying to set my preferences for the college entrance exam. I had limited information about different majors. I did not know what I would do once I got a degree. My primary source of knowledge was some good friends. I ended up going to the college of my first choice. However, in reality, it was not my choice; it was the choice of my guiding friends. If I had better guidance, I would have taken a different path. In graduate school, the decisions I made were not well-informed. I feel that I lost a lot in my life because of being deprived of proper guidance to have a meaningful educational and career trajectory.

Meaningless, but mandatory

During my life journey, sometimes I would experience a lack of meaning out of necessity. For instance, I made up my mind to go to college at an early age. However, I had to go to vocational school to get a job to support myself. The vocational school curriculum was designed to produce nurses. For the college entrance exam, I had to study many topics that were not covered at the school.

Furthermore, since I had no intention to continue my career as a nurse, I was not entirely dedicated to the school. I learned everything half-heartedly, thinking that I would go to college and change to a completely different major. Later on, when I was working as a nurse and attending college, I had no ambition to succeed at work. I was just doing the minimum to survive until I graduated from college.

Another example of a meaningless experience was my military service. When I graduated from college, I was supposed to do my mandatory military service for six months. I did not want to because I did not believe that I would learn in six months how to be a soldier and to fight the enemy. Culturally, fulfilling military service was considered a duty to the homeland. To me, it was not patriotic to do military service. It was just a waste of time and resources. I tried to use all legal excuses to postpone my service. Then, my dream came through. The government made a one-time exception to allow payment of around eight thousand dollars to do the service for only one month rather than six months. I took the opportunity and paid to be exempted. For me, even one month was painful because it was complete nonsense. I learned almost nothing. I did nothing meaningful to help my homeland through that service. It was a waste of time. Perhaps, the only meaningful lesson was to learn the importance of meaning in life.

Meaningless addictions

Bad habits or addiction are good examples of meaningless events in life. If we examine all life, we will find many such meaningless events. I want to share one of mine. I began following soccer games when I was in middle school. Like many in Turkey, I took a side. I had my sports team. I would spend several hours a week following the games, reading the news, and discussing the outcome with peers. I would feel great joy whenever my team won. I would feel really sad whenever it lost. I remember that I would listen to the radio broadcast of the games during the weekend in a freezing room since in the warm room, kids were destroying my concentration. For a few years, I never questioned the meaning of what I was doing. To me, it was just a pleasant experience. After all, almost everyone I knew had a similar habit. Later on, in my high school years, when I began reading and reflecting on my life, I realized that following soccer games for hours was utterly meaningless for me. Since I was not even a soccer player, I had nothing to gain from following the soccer games. Thus, I decided to give up this habit altogether. I never regretted my decision. I no longer follow any soccer games. I see no meaning in doing so. I accept that it gives momentary pleasure within the hedonic dimension. However, once we move to the eudemonic dimension, we will have difficulty to justify spending that much time to gain a fleeting positive feeling.

Meaningless habits

Another example of meaningless habit is following news on TV, printed media, or the Internet. I began following the news once I was first exposed to the TV while attending middle school. At that time, I thought that it was an enlightening experience. I would digest all kinds of news without filtering. I had no idea that some of it might have been slanted. Over time, it became a routine of my life to get a good dose of daily news. There was a fixed hour of a news program in the evening. We did not have to follow the news around the hour as it is the case now. Out of curiosity, we have an urge to follow the news. However, it is hard to claim that the benefit is worth the cost. Therefore, it is hard to be satisfied when we reflect and realize that we are wasting our time (life) on consuming news. The more we feel we waste our time on such a useless habit, the less we feel satisfied with life. Yes, it is painful to have bad (or meaningless) habits. However, it is not easy to change them. As I moved in the eudemonic dimension, I had to struggle a lot to get rid of those hedonic habits as I became dissatisfied with their fleeting pleasure.

Meaningless waiting

Sometimes, the society in which we live imposes meaninglessness on us. For instance, when I moved to Saudi Arabia, I soon began experiencing meaningless waiting whenever I had to receive any governmental approval. Indeed, one of the first words I learned in Arabic was "bukrah" which means "tomorrow." I would hear this word again and again from government officials. Later on, I realized that the cultural meaning of "bukrah" is different from its dictionary meaning. Bukrah sometimes means next week, or next month, or even never coming. I had many experiences with meaningless waiting. It was meaningless because it did not have to be. For me, it was a complete waste of time to go several times for a job to be done. Perhaps, the only benefit of such meaningless waiting was to give me an unforgettable lesson that meaninglessness is great pain. Of course, over time, the diminishing marginal utility helps to lessen the pain. However, you could not avoid feeling the pain whenever you experienced the meaningless event.

Accomplishment and Disappointment Phase

I have many experiences in which meaning truly enriched my life satisfaction. If we use a food analogy, meaning from having, doing, and being would be nutrition while pleasure would be spices. Though we receive immediate pleasure if we have our favorite spices, we will be satisfied with food only if it provides the necessary nutrition. I have learned that lasting life satisfaction is possible through meaning both short term and long term. In the short term, we need to bring meaning to our daily works. In the long run, we should have a sense of direction about what we aim to accomplish in our life.

Meaning through reading

In high school, when I began reading books for the sake of gaining knowledge, I realized that I should examine the meaning of all events in my life. That is when I attempted to give up some meaningless habits I had. As I was expanding my knowledge, I felt that I was expanding my world. I remember that I read only one book beyond textbooks during my elementary and secondary education. I fell in love with reading in my first year of high school. After reading a few hundred books while in high school, I realized that being rich in knowledge is as important as being rich in money. Thus, it was wrong to see knowledge as just a means for making more money. I realized that my personal world was made from my perceived understanding of the actual world. The only way for me to enrich my perceived world was through knowledge.

As stated before, the meaning is the food for the mind. We cannot be satisfied by feeding the body and stomach alone. We need to provide food for the mind as well. The stomach has a limited capacity; therefore, we feel full once we eat one or two plates of food. The mind is always hungrily looking for food. Indeed, as long as we are awake, we cannot stop thinking. The mind is always occupied with something. The mind is satisfied if we have something meaningful. Therefore, if we provide food for the mind in our life, we will likely receive higher satisfaction from having, doing, and being. Indeed, meaning could even convert our painful experience into a pleasant one.

Money for meaningful activities

In high school, I learned from some good friends that virtue could bring even higher life satisfaction. A friend of mine preferred to spend his own money to pay for my college prep school rather than engaging in personal consumption.

He did it out of his virtuous character without expecting anything in return. Obviously, he had forgone the pleasure of having and doing something with that money. Since it was an entirely voluntary choice from his side, he must have received higher pleasure in thinking that he was helping a friend to have the opportunity to give better fruit in life. Actually, his parents were not wealthy. His father was sending him a monthly stipend to spend on his necessities. I even heard that once his daddy sent him money to buy shoes. He preferred to spend that money on my school fee while keeping his old and ripped shoes. Given the competitiveness of the college exam, it could not have been possible to pass if I had not gone to the college prep school. Till today, I still remember this friend and feel that I owe my entire career to him, to a certain extent.

Since I got my very first job, I have been providing support to needy students. I receive great pleasure in helping students to flourish who have great potential, but few resources. Actually, for me, helping those students gives much higher pleasure than spending money on my hedonic pleasure. Several friends and I even established an association to provide support to needy students in a more professional manner. Every year, we provide a scholarship to high school and college students. I confess that it is not easy to cut from your own expenses and give to strangers. However, when I reflect on my expenses in the past, I never regret the money I have spent on such a good cause. I feel great joy from doing that. I realize that the pleasure of personal consumption is limited to time consumption. However, the pleasure of spending for others could last, as we remember.

Meaningful vs. moneyful career

I have seen the importance of meaning in pursuing my educational path and career. Once I considered education as the necessary means, I began ascribing meaning to anything that helped me to get a better grade. As discussed above, it was not easy to find a direction in life. Perhaps, I wasted half of my life to be what others wanted me to be in my educational and career journey. Once I graduated from college, I decided to stay in academia to have more freedom to determine my life. Despite its economic attractiveness, I did not choose bureaucracy because it was too rigid in controlling the lives of individuals. To me, meaningful life starts with a certain sense of autonomy. Being controlled by others is a form of slavery. By our nature, we are born to live a free life. We do not like to be enslaved in any way.

However, it was not easy for me to gain true freedom in my academic career. In my early career in Turkey, I soon realized that a form of slavery also existed within academia. Academic titles were being used as a means for oppression. Similar to the military system, full professors were like four-star generals while graduate assistants were academic slaves. The only difference was that the system allowed movement from the bottom to the top as long as you played your role at each level. Of course, as a slave, you were not supposed to object to your master. I remember once I expressed my disagreement with my professor on a political issue. He spent two hours to cleanse my mind to make sure that I accepted his view on the matter. Did he succeed? Not at all. He did not know that the door of the human ear can only be opened from the inside.

Obviously, I was not happy with what I found in academia in Turkey. I decided to look for an opportunity to move abroad for a better academic life. I was a doctoral candidate in one doctoral program and had just completed my coursework for the second doctoral program in Turkey when I received a scholarship to earn a Ph.D. in the United States. Despite my progress in Turkey, I decided to move to the United States without hesitation. I had to restart work on my third doctoral degree from scratch. It was a waste of at least two years. I did not think that way. I felt that it would save the rest of my life because it was going to free me from academic slavery in Turkey.

Indeed, I found a great degree of freedom in the United States. The academic hierarchy was relatively non-existent. Professors approached their graduate students as mental partners. Rather than filling the minds of students with their great wisdom, they would try to open their minds. Therefore, my academic journey in the United States was more meaningful and enjoyable. Of course, it was not the perfect freedom to flourish. As I began forming my research interest and publication portfolio, I felt limited in freedom. I decided to pursue an unorthodox path in economics. That is when I saw specific resistance within mainstream economics. Getting published in a high-ranking established journal was almost impossible. Until I got my promotion to associate professor, I had to publish and teach subjects that were not my first choice. I did that mainly to score points for the promotion. It was OK, but not quite a pleasant experience. Once I had enough publications for my promotion, I began feeling the freedom to work on topics that were dear to my mind and heart. That is how I realized that a meaningful career is one that is driven by my intrinsic desire rather than external demand.

Teaching or touching to the mind and heart

I have experienced the great pleasure of injecting meaning into my teaching, as well. I have taught many different courses throughout my career. The most enjoyable were those I developed based on my research and intellectual interest. I never felt any burden in preparing and delivering those courses. I found them helpful for myself as much as for my students. Actually, to me, the most fun part of teaching is the opportunity to touch the heart of students through sharing what you think is essential in life. Passing textbook information without adding passionate life lessons is dry and dull from my perspective. Therefore, I always try to present some life stories or inspirational quotes as little brain exercises to warm up for the lecture and make lessons meaningful. I have seen, again and again, that students are eager to learn a subject if they think it is useful for their personal or professional life.

My highest satisfaction from teaching comes from seeing an intellectual awakening among my students. Of course, that does not happen often. However, having one or two students each year experience such a transformation gives me great pleasure. That is when I feel that I am making a meaningful contribution to humanity. To me, a student resembles a seed with enormous potential. Indeed, all technological devices are the fruit of someone who was provided great support to flourish. Thus, when I see the fruit of my teaching in the form of transforming students to realize their potential, I receive enormous pleasure. I argue that for good teachers, such pleasure is even more rewarding than a financial one.

Enriching life with meaningful engagements

Once I found meaning to be necessary for life satisfaction, I began looking for a way to add meaning to my daily life events. I found great value in inserting meaning to almost everything in my life. For instance, for me, the best breakfast is not the one with the most delicious food. Instead, it is the one with delicious food for the stomach and the mind. Thus, I would rather learn something by watching or listening while having breakfast. I do not enjoy going to a restaurant just to enjoy a good meal. Instead, I prefer to go to a restaurant with my family or friends to enjoy food and spend good time together.

What I found was that many boring life experiences could be pleasant if we add some meaning. For instance, as a frequent flyer, I found great pleasure in flying because I always have a plan to use my flying time fruitfully. While driving, I listen to interesting podcasts to enhance my knowledge. Whenever I have to wait for someone, I read rather than counting the minutes to kill my neurons. Indeed, even when I am on vacation, I feel relaxing alone is boring and tiresome. I need to add a meaningful outcome to my vacation to enjoy it better. In short, hunger to the stomach is boredom to the mind. When we feel hungry, we eat to feed the body; whenever we feel bored, we should provide meaning to feed the mind.

Enhancing our knowledge is the key to enrich life with meaning. That is because through knowledge, we can penetrate higher meaning and esthetics. Thus, knowledge works like light, revealing hidden beauty and meaning. In a video interview[7], Richard Feynman, the Nobel Prize-winning theoretical physicist, gave a great example to explain how we enrich our life through knowledge:

"I have a friend who's an artist and has sometimes taken a view which I don't agree with very well. He'll hold up a flower and say, "look how beautiful it is," and I'll agree. Then he says, "I as an artist can see how beautiful this is but you as a scientist take this all apart and it becomes a dull thing," and I think that he's kind of nutty. First of all, the beauty that he sees is available to other people and to me too, I believe. Although I may not be quite as refined aesthetically as he is … I can appreciate the beauty of a flower. At the same time, I see much more about the flower than he sees. I could imagine the cells in there, the complicated actions inside, which also have a beauty. I mean it's not just beauty at this dimension, at one centimeter; there's also beauty at smaller dimensions, the inner structure, also the processes. The fact that the colors in the

---

7   https://www.youtube.com/watch?v=ZbFM3rn4ldo

flower evolved in order to attract insects to pollinate it is interesting; it means that insects can see the color. It adds a question: does this aesthetic sense also exist in the lower forms? Why is it aesthetic? All kinds of interesting questions which the science knowledge only adds to the excitement, the mystery and the awe of a flower. It only adds. I don't understand how it subtracts."

Another Nobel Laureate in physics, Frank Wilczek, in *A Beautiful Question*, made a compelling argument that beauty is the essence of the entire creation. He stated his question as follows in the beginning of the book: "If an energetic and powerful Creator made the world, it could be that what moved Him- or Her, or Them, or It, to create was precisely an impulse to make something beautiful" (Wilczek 2016, 2). Later on, he mentioned symmetry at the micro and macro levels as compelling evidence for beauty. As Feynman rightly stated, such beauty is only accessible to knowledgeable people. As the light reveals the beauty in physical objects, enlightenment through gaining knowledge reveals abstract beauty in terms of meaning in the cosmic phenomena.

Indeed, I argue that due to the meaning, we endure many challenges and pain in life. For instance, for those who pursue hedonic happiness, committing to a family life might not make any sense. It is better to be free from the burden of raising children when pursuing the sensual pleasure of relationships. That is why marriage and raising children are in decline in modern times. However, if we think raising children is a meaningful contribution to humanity, we will endure the hardship for the sake of fruitful outcome.

Conclusion

Including meaning dimension into the happiness equation did bring higher satisfaction. Indeed, throughout my educational and career life, I have found meaning to be the boosting element for life satisfaction. The meaning was more enriching than money in bringing happiness. Even when I had to endure something to make money or get promoted, I have tried to insert some meaning to make it a more pleasant experience. I even made a list of several meaningful outcomes in my career. When I feel a little depressed, I remind myself of those outcomes to feel satisfied and happy. It is true, as I bring meaning to my life, I receive higher satisfaction. However, the search for higher meaning leads to a dead end when I begin asking about the ultimate meaning of life. I felt that Spinoza was right when he famously said, "…experience had taught me that all the things which regularly occur in ordinary life are empty and futile". In other words, there is an end to the temporal meaning as shown below:

Figure 2. DEAD Loop of Happiness with Meaning

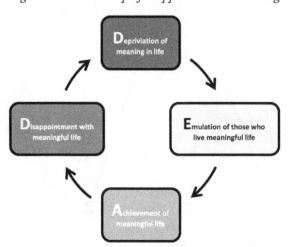

As seen in Figure 3, the marginal utility of meaning is very different from that of having, doing, and being at the hedonic dimension. Meaning adds a new dimension. Thus, we will be seeking happiness in two dimensions. In one-dimensional happiness, we go forward and backward along the same line. In two-dimensional happiness, the meaning is like height. We can go up and down. Unlike hedonic happiness, we argue that the marginal utility from eudemonic happiness is increasing. As we enhance in meaning, we derive increasing marginal utility. For instance, if we think it is pointless to seek sensual pleasure without knowing the meaning of life, we need to seek knowledge. As we learn more in our intellectual quest, we gain even higher pleasure. If we are reading an interesting book, the more we read and understand, the more pleasure we will receive. Thus, unlike bodily pleasure, intellectual pleasure is upsloping. It begins with a low marginal utility. It gets higher and higher. We argue the decreasing rate of bodily (sensual) pleasure is due to the limitations of the body. Since there is almost no limit to our intellectual capacity, we can almost never be full in our quest for knowledge. Of course, we get tired while seeking knowledge. That is again due to our biological limits. Thus, we think that as we find more answers to our existential questions, we will get increasingly happier. However, this will not last forever.

Figure 3. Long-term Marginal Utility of Meaningful Life

In short, as we realize our utility from meaning is also doomed to approach zero over time, our life satisfaction will also approach to zero. In other words, our marginal happiness function of H_{el} = U (H, D, B, L) + M (H, D, B, L) is going to approach to zero over time:

$$\Delta H_{el} \rightarrow 0 \text{ as } \Delta U \rightarrow 0 \text{ and } \Delta M \rightarrow 0$$

As we question the meaning of what we do, we might realize that everything is ultimately meaningless if there is no life after death. Assuming no afterlife, our total utility based on utility and meaning from having, doing, being, will also become zero with death, which has an increasing probability as we age. We need to look for an alternative route to avoid desperation and depression.

Chapter 9

Searching for Eudemonic Happiness Through Believing

"Happiness is neither within us nor without us, it is the union of ourselves with God."

—Blaise Pascal

Introduction

Belief in a Supreme Being who created the universe and is capable to sustain it forever is a great addition to the happiness equation. For some people, belief is a key to another dimension while for others, it is an expansion of the meaning dimension. It helps them to make better sense of reality, life, death, and beyond. In this chapter, we will discuss belief as an interactive term within the eudemonic dimension of happiness. Later, we will explore belief as the key to the transcendental dimension of happiness.

The Caveman Story

To better understand the role of belief in our life, let's reflect on a very famous and old story. It is a metaphorical one told by Plato over two thousand years ago. The story of cavemen. In his book, *The Republic*, Plato asked us to imagine a cave where some people have been imprisoned from birth. They are chained by legs and necks to make sure that they can gaze only at the wall in front of them. They can see neither each other nor even their own bodies. Behind the prisoners, a fire burns with continuous flames. A walkway is between the prisoners and the fire. Thus, the fire produces shadows of any object passing on the sidewalk. The prisoners see nothing but shadows. They think the shadow is real. For instance, if a goat is passing by, the prisoners would see the shadow of a goat. They would hear the sound as well. They link sound to shadows and think the sound comes from shadows. After telling the story, Plato asks us to guess whether it is possible for the prisoners to know the reality behind the shadows as long as they are chained. Actually, knowing the reality is to find an answer to an existential question regarding the shadows. Therefore, knowledge of the shadows is strongly linked to life satisfaction.

We think the cave allegory works well to explain our multi-dimensional happiness model. Obviously, for the prisoners, the shadow is the reality. They know nothing beyond the shadow. Thus, their happiness is the function of having, doing, being, and meaning through their perceived reality. Now, assume that one of the prisoners pursues happiness through accumulating shadows. He chases shadows on the wall with his eyes and counts them as his own property. He has a powerful memory to keep track of his belongings. After many years, he ends up having thousands of goats, sheep, cows, etc. He considers himself the real owner of those shadowy objects. He is proud of his wealth. He even thinks that he is better than other lazy prisoners. Is it possible to count him happy and satisfied? Not at all. Why? It is because we know that shadows cannot bring us real satisfaction. It is nothing but ultimate self-deception.

In reality, the cave is the material/physical world in which we are born. We are no different from those prisoners. We are bounded to live within certain physical laws and space. Like the prisoners, we do not see the ultimate reality behind the shadowy existence of material objects. Thus, we think of shadowy physical objects as reality. If we do not penetrate into the colorful (meaningful) reality behind the observed shadowy phenomena, we would consider life to be dull and boring.

The good news is that since Descartes, we are well aware of the difference between observed phenomena and ultimate reality. We have learned that colors are nothing but different wavelengths of light. Similarly, the entire material reality is nothing but a wave-like shadowy emergence within the vast ocean of the subatomic world. It is evident that what we see is only our perception of reality, not the reality itself. We are bounded to have a certain perception of the universe. However, through science and philosophy, we clearly know that reality is different from our perception. Thus, we face a similar challenge as the prisoners: (how) can we know the reality? How can we set ourselves free from the chains?

Faith and freedom

For some people, faith is a way to free ourselves from the cave of the material world and see the reality behind the desired shadows. There are two ways to go beyond the shadows. One is to believe in the reality beyond shadows in the form of a wish without any verified evidence. The other way is to study the shadow and find convincing evidence for the transcendental reality. We call those in the first category "skeptical believers" because they are not sure about the ultimate reality, therefore, they seek satisfaction in worldly things. We call those in the second category "transcendental believers" because they transcend beyond the observed phenomenal reality and pursue satisfaction through something beyond this world (transcendental). Skeptical believers might believe in life after death; however, they live their life as if there is no life beyond this world. If God and hereafter are real, they are ignorant of this reality, like those who deny any reality. Therefore, their ultimate objective is to seek satisfaction in this world. Transcendental believers have conviction about the reality based on verified evidence or self-conviction. For the first group, faith brings certain additional comfort; for the second group, faith brings transcendental transformation.

Faith and Happiness for Skeptical Believers

For skeptical believers, faith is an interactive term in the happiness equation increasing the temporal meaning. In other words, they seek satisfaction in this world with utility and meaning from worldly having, doing, being, and believing as an interactive term for meaning. Using the cave metaphor, they believe that there is a reality behind the shadows but are pursuing happiness by chasing shadows similar to everyone else. Thus, the belief brings some relief by helping to ignore the pain associated with death. However, it does not change the attitude toward worldly life because it is just blind faith, not firm conviction. Therefore, they still have a eudemonic happiness equation with an added interactive term of believing as shown below:

$$H_{e2} = U\ (H,\ D,\ B,\ L)\ +M\ (H,\ D,\ B,\ L)\ +(F_s{}^*M)$$

Faith is helpful in terms of adding meaning and gaining utility from having, doing, and being. Without faith, one has to accept the reality that everything is doomed to be annihilated at any moment. Thus, thinking of death as the ultimate destroyer would destroy the utility from having, doing, and being as long as we think of death. Even blind faith helps skeptical believers to skip thinking of death by accepting the idea that life continues after death. Thus, faith works like insurance against death. Believing that they have insurance helps them to think that their efforts are not fruitless (meaningless). As long as they forget the reality of death through their blind faith, they will enjoy their lives without too much concern about the painful end at any moment.

Many people have realized that having faith is good for higher happiness. Tolstoy was one of them. In his search for happiness, he concluded that for a happy life, one must have faith. However, this was not a blind faith. For Tolstoy, "Faith is the knowledge of the meaning of human life…Faith is the power of life. If a man lives, he believes in something." Faith is important because only through faith can one find the meaning of life by overcoming the problem of death and ultimate annihilation: "The faith may be, and whatever answers it may give, and to whomsoever it gives them, every such answer gives to the finite existence of man an infinite meaning, a meaning not destroyed by sufferings, deprivations,

Figure 1. Eudemonic Happiness Dimensions with Having,
Doing, Being, Loving, Meaning, and Believing(s)

or death. This means that only in faith can we find for life a meaning and a possibility."

Shadow and satisfaction

Using the cave metaphor, we think faith is to know the meaning of shadows. It is to know the reality behind the shadows. Of course, it is to live in line with this belief. Thus, we agree with Tolstoy that skeptical believers cannot reach full life satisfaction. Even though belief brings them certain relief, they are doomed to experience the ultimate dissatisfaction in life. Indeed, once Tolstoy concluded that faith is the only path to real life satisfaction, he explored the deeds of the religious establishment (the Church). He found it insincere and fake: "These believers of our circle, just like myself, living insufficiency and superfluity, tried to increase or preserve them, feared privations, suffering, and death, and just like myself and all of us unbelievers, lived to satisfy their desires, and lived just as bad, if not worse, than the unbelievers...." He denounced the Church and turned toward "the believers among the poor, simple, unlettered folk: pilgrims, monks, sectarians, and peasants."

Religious, but secular

The key difference between skeptical believers and transcendental believers is that the former pursues life satisfaction in this world while the latter thinks it is not possible to be satisfied with anything or everything in this world. This is very much in line with a comprehensive definition of secularization by Charles Taylor

(2007). In his masterpiece, *A Secular Age*, Taylor made a forceful argument that most religious people are actually secular. He gave three definitions of secularity. First, it is the separation of church and state. Second, it is the diminishing importance of religion in social life. Third, it is the pursuit of satisfaction in this world. In his view, anyone who pursues satisfaction in this world is worldly (secular). He claimed that in the past, religious Christians did not believe that you could reach satisfaction in this world even if you have everything you want. They used to believe that life satisfaction is possible through something that transcends this world. Thus, their objective was not to seek satisfaction in this world. They had a certain mission to fulfill in life. They would be happier with what would come beyond this life.

Within the cave analogy, Taylor's argument means that pursuing satisfaction through shadows is to be secular. In other words, if one believes the reality behind the shadows, one has to have a different attitude toward the shadows. A person who knows shadows and the reality behind with a sense of certainty could not be satisfied with shadows. He/she would not engage in the pursuit of shadows like the chained prisoner. Indeed, in Plato's story, one of the prisoners would manage to escape from the cave. He would initially be blind to the reality, given the intensity of the light. Once his eyes were adjusted to the light, he would see the reality behind the shadows he knew in the cave. He would feel sorry about his time lost not knowing the reality. He would pity his friends. He would go back to the cave to correct their belief. When he got into the cave, he would be blinded for a while again due to the adjustment from the light to the darkness. He would begin telling his friends the truth behind the observed shadows. He wanted to help them by freeing them from the cave. Of course, the friends could not digest this radical change in their perceived reality. They had lived their entire life pursuing the shadows. They did not want to know that their efforts gave them nothing but deception. They rejected the suggested reality and claimed that their friend lost his mind when he got out of the cave. The prisoners, according to Plato, would infer from the freed man's blindness that the journey out of the cave had harmed him and that they should not undertake a similar journey.

Conclusion

We argue that it is inevitable to ask some existential questions as we seek happiness through meaning after failing to find happiness in the hedonic dimension. As we see people around us claiming to find happiness through spirituality, we will explore a suitable one if we are not completely biased toward faith. We will find life to be more meaningful with a spiritual path as long as we think it has answers to our existential questions. However, we cannot avoid questioning the authenticity of the answers. Though Dostoevsky famously said that he would prefer Christ with the promise of eternity rather than truth without eternity, it seems that, in modern times, many people prefer so-called scientific truth over Christ. As Charles Taylor said, if we do not have verified belief, we might fear that our strong desire for God, or for eternity, "might after all be self-induced illusion that materialists claim to be" (Taylor 2007, chap. 16). If we do not have compelling evidence showing that we are indeed on the right path, we will eventually sink into doubt and desperation due to overwhelming atheistic messages around us, as shown below.

Figure 2. DEAD Loop of Happiness with Skeptical Faith

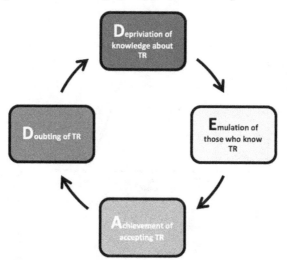

We argue that marginal utility from spiritual experience is also upsloping. As we deepen in spiritual experience, we derive higher utility. It brings more meaning to our daily life. As shown in Figure 3, seeking spiritual experience shifts our marginal utility to the right. When we become more spiritual, we gain higher utility. That is because our faith will give us wishful hope about the eternal outcome of our daily endeavors. As long as we believe in that, we will consider our life more meaningful. However, if we eventually question our faith and begin falling into doubt about its authenticity, we will hit the dead end. Our marginal utility will diminish to zero.

In short, as we realize that our utility from having, doing, being, meaning, and believing is doomed to approach zero over time, our life satisfaction will also approach zero. In other words, our happiness function of $H_{e2} = U$ (H, D, B, M, Fs) is going to approach to zero over time:

$$\Delta H_{e2} \to 0 \text{ as } \Delta U \to 0$$

Figure 3. Long-term Marginal Utility of Secular Spirituality

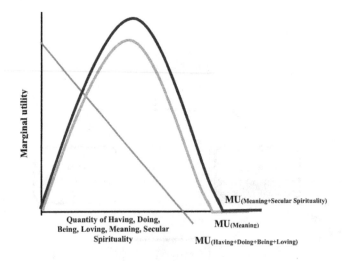

Chapter 10

Scientific Research of Eudemonic Happiness

"Happiness can be found even in the darkest of times, if one only remembers to turn on the light."
—**Harry Potter** and the *Prisoner of Azkaban* (2004)

Introduction

Though the eudemonic dimension of happiness has been around since the time of Aristotle, only recently have we begun to explore the topic through scientific measurement. Particularly, with the rise of positive psychology, we have seen growing attempts to quantify different domains of life, including a sense of purpose or meaning, kindness, curiosity, autonomy, sense of humor, self-esteem, and aesthetic appreciation (Kashdan 2004). Each of these domains has been found to be positively correlated with subjective wellbeing. For instance, Sirgy et al. (2011) studied the effect of travel on various life domains, including leisure/recreational life, family life, love life, spiritual life, intellectual life, and the self. They developed a model to measure the effect of travel on all of those domains that they consider to be essential in enhancing one's overall well-being. Sirgy (2012) also published a book discussing different domains of life. These findings provide indirect evidence for the importance of eudemonic dimension of happiness.

Intrinsic Aspirations and Eudemonic Happiness

As discussed in Chapter 6, many studies have sought to understand the importance of extrinsic and intrinsic aspirations in life. Intrinsic goals are assumed to help individuals to have a fulfilled life through expanded self-knowledge and deeper connections with others, as suggested by the eudemonic happiness. Conventional intrinsic goals include personal acceptance or growth, emotional affiliation, and community feeling while extrinsic goals include financial success, image or physical attractiveness, and social fame or popularity. They are a way to fulfill the innate needs defined by self-determination theory. For instance, emotional affiliation and community feeling are driven by relatedness whereas self-acceptance is driven by competence. The desire to fulfill one's inner needs is autonomous, meaning it overlaps with the need for autonomy.

According to self-determination theory, the primary motivation behind life goals and actions is to satisfy certain needs. In this context, intrinsic goals are driven toward satisfying three basic psychological needs: autonomy, relatedness, and competence (Deci and Ryan 2000). Autonomy refers to the feeling that our choices in life are driven by our own free will rather than being imposed or coerced by others (DeCharms 1968). Relatedness refers to feeling that we are related or connected to those who are important to us rather than being alienated(Baumeister and Leary 1995). Finally, competence refers to the feeling that we have an innate ability to effectively manage our life rather than being ineffective and incompetent(White 1995). Thus, the fulfillment of essential needs is a universal quest for human well-being through the eudemonic dimension.

According to self-determination theories, the immoderate pursuit of extrinsic aspirations is associated with lower SWB while the pursuit of intrinsic aspiration is linked to higher SWB (Fromm 1976) Although extrinsic goals can be a means for the fulfillment of basic needs, if they become too important relative to intrinsic goals, they are likely to result in negative SWB (Sheldon et al. 2004). Past research has revealed that when a person places more importance on extrinsic goals compared to intrinsic goals, it results in lower SWB. Many studies have confirmed that intrinsic values relate to higher life satisfaction and happiness (Kasser and Ryan 2001; Ryan et al. 1999). These findings have been replicated in many countries.

Success and Failure of Capitalism

Although global capitalism based on materialistic values has been very successful in producing an enormous amount of wealth, it has failed to deliver authentic happiness. People might be wealthier, but they are not happier and healthier, as expected. We think that this paradox is the product of an overemphasis on the hedonic dimension of happiness at the cost of other dimensions.

In his book, *The Hedonistic Imperative*, David Pearce (2015) argued that we are near to "an engineered paradise" through a "transhuman" generation. Using the subtitle of "heaven on earth?" he made the following bold prediction for achieving heaven on earth through science and technology: "nanotechnology and genetic engineering will eliminate aversive experience from the living world. Over the next thousand years or so, the biological substrates of suffering will be eradicated completely. 'Physical' and 'mental' pain alike are destined to disappear into evolutionary history. The biochemistry of everyday discontents will be genetically phased out too. Malaise will be replaced by the biochemistry of bliss. Matter and energy will be sculpted into life-loving super-beings animated by gradients of well-being. The states of mind of our descendants are likely to be incomprehensibly diverse by comparison with today. Yet all will share at least one common feature: sublime and all-pervasive happiness."

No doubt that capitalism has been successful in production and consumption. However, it has failed to bring the promised paradise. According to Karl Polanyi (1957), the free market system dehumanizes human beings by turning them and their natural environment to "fictitious commodities." He argued that the system alienates and separates human beings from both their surroundings and from their own powers that they exercise in their life activity. This commodification process turns human beings in society into homo-economics. In other words, the free market system destroys the noneconomic and social nature of man and turns him into an individual who acts from only two motives, the fear of starvation and the hope of profit. It serves the hedonic dimension while ignoring the eudemonic dimension of happiness.

Meaning of Consumption

The means-end chain theory suggests that consumer behavior is either consciously or unconsciously goal-directed (Reynolds, Gutman, & Institute for Consumer Research, 1986). Consumers buy goods to achieve certain goals that are shaped by personal, social or moral values behind the desire to be happy, to belong, to protect, to be useful, and so on. The attributes of goods are the "means," and values are the "ends" that consumers would like to achieve. The theory of reasoned action suggests that consumers behave according to their attitudes and beliefs about the outcome of their behavior and the relative importance (value) they assign to the outcome (Fishbein & Ajzen, 1975).

We consume goods not only to fulfill our functional needs but also for what they represent to us and others. The goods play a vital symbolic role in our lives in communicating personal, social, and cultural messages (McCracken, 1988). In a consumer society, consumption is to some extent linked to personal and collective identity, confirming what was famously put by William James: "A man's Self is the total of all that he can call his, not only his body and his psychic powers but his clothes, his friends, his wife and children, his ancestors, his reputation and works, his lands and yacht and bank account..."(James, 1950, p.291-292).

Empty Selves vs. Full Shelves

In a modern consumer society, individuals are in a continuous process of constructing their personal identity through consuming material goods as social and cultural symbols. Cushman (1990) said that the "empty self" of a consumer is constantly in need of "filling up" through material consumption. Companies are quite successful in providing positional goods and services to conspicuous consumers. They do not sell "just" products; they sell brands, prestige, visions, dreams, associations, status, etc. (Klein, 2001).

Indeed, some might argue that capitalism makes people prefer being a satisfied animal rather than a dissatisfied human being. Those who are affected by conspicuous consumer culture live in the hedonic dimension perceiving fun/pleasure as the primary, if not the only, purpose of their lives. From the eudemonic perspective, being a human being is always preferable even if that means a life full of misery because happiness is defined based on flourishing and meaningful life, not sheer pleasure.

In his famous hypothetical thought experiment, Nozick asked us to imagine a machine that could make us feel whatever desirable or pleasurable experiences we would like to have.[8] After all, according to neuroscience, the feeling is just the outcome of chemical reactions in our brain. Assuming that neuropsychologists find out a way to stimulate our brain to create pleasurable experiences that are not different than the ones induced by real-life experiences, Nozick then asked, would we prefer to hook up to the experience machine over real life experience? Nozick argued that if we value pleasure as the only desired outcome from life, we would prefer the machine. However, he said, people pursue something more than pleasure in life. Therefore, they would not choose the machine.

Perhaps, we do not need to be hypothetical anymore because capitalism has created not one, but many experience machines such as circuses, concerts, musical theatre, amusement parks, funfairs, films, theme parks, discotheques, broadcasting media, video games, etc. While many people around the world are hooking up to these machines every day.

Full vs. Empty Life

We recently have seen more studies directly measuring the eudemonic dimension and its impact on subjective wellbeing. For instance, Peterson et al. (2005) developed 18 questions for three different orientations to happiness. They used the following questions to capture the meaning orientation:

- My life serves a higher purpose.
- In choosing what to do, I always consider whether it will benefit other people.

---

8   Nozick, Robert. *Anarchy, State, and Utopia.* Basic Books, New York, 1974, pp. 42–45.

- I have a responsibility to make the world a better place.
- My life has a lasting meaning.
- What I do matters to society.

In addition to the meaning orientation, the above study also explored pleasure and engagement orientations to happiness. The survey data of 845 participants revealed that those who scored high in all three orientations had a higher happiness score. Similarly, those who scored lower in all three orientations had a lower happiness score. The authors concluded that the three orientations are complementary in the pursuit of happiness.

Anic and Toncic (2013) confirmed the same findings in their study of nearly 700 students who rated their life satisfaction, positive and negative affect, orientations to happiness, and self-control. The study grouped the participants into four groups based on their responses: students who highly endorsed hedonic and eudemonic orientation were considered to live "the full life" while those who did not endorse either were considered to live the "empty life". The study revealed that people who live a full life are the happiest, they value intrinsic life goals and have good self-control.

Findings from our research on eudemonic happiness

In 2013, we conducted an extensive survey in Istanbul, Turkey, to compare the roles of intrinsic and extrinsic aspirations in subjective wellbeing[9]. The survey participants were randomly recruited across all 20 districts in Istanbul based on the local population. Our study reproduced the well-known aspiration index (AI) capturing 11 domains of human experience: self-acceptance, affiliation, community feeling, security, health, spirituality, financial success, image, popularity, hedonism, and conformity (Kasser et al. 2007). The questions related to the 11 domains were largely from the AI survey, with some modifications made based on cultural differences. Our survey added three domains—namely, intellectual life, honesty and fairness, and aesthetic appreciation. From the survey data, we measured the relative importance of each value/goal within the entire

9   For further information, please refer to my published paper: "Psycho-Economic Aspiration and Subjective Wellbeing: Evidence from a representative Turkish Sample", *International Journal of Social Economics*, *Vol. 44, Iss:6*, doi: 10.1108/IJSE-11-2015-0312

value/goal system through the mean-corrected importance scores, one for each type of aspiration. We also assessed the life satisfaction through the Satisfaction with Life Scale (SWLS) (Diener et al. 1985).

The Hypotheses Tested

In our study, we aimed to test several hypotheses related to one's goals in life and eudemonic happiness. First hypothesis (H1) proposed that a direct positive relationship exists between honesty and fairness and subjective wellbeing (SWB). This hypothesis was weakly supported by the survey analysis. The correlation coefficient was positive, but small and statistically significant, providing weak evidence for validating H1.

H2 proposed that aesthetic appreciation was positively related to SWB. This hypothesis was also partially validated by the data. The correlation coefficient was small, but positive and statistically significant, providing weak evidence for confirming H2. The coefficients for this variable in the regression models were found to be statistically insignificant.

H3 proposed that a direct positive relationship exists between a relatively rich intellectual life and SWB. This hypothesis was strongly supported by both correlation and regression results. The correlation coefficient was positive, relatively high, and statistically significant. Likewise, the coefficient for the intellectual life domain in all regression models turned out to be positive and statistically significant.

H4 proposed that a direct positive relationship exists between intrinsic, self-transcendent life domains and SWB. Intrinsic life domains were strongly related to higher SWB based on both evidence from relevant correlation coefficients and regression results. Likewise, self-transcendent life domains (intellectual life, spirituality, and conformity) were strongly related to higher SWB. Indeed, the regression model with aggregate intrinsic and self-transcendent life domains clearly revealed the positive contribution of all intrinsic and self-transcendent values overall to SWB, providing strong evidence for the validation of H4.

H5 proposed that a direct negative relationship exists between extrinsic, physical-self life domains and SWB. This hypothesis was mostly supported. Correlation coefficients for all three extrinsic domains (money, fame, and image) were insignificant, showing no statistically significant relationship between those values and SWB. Likewise, the relative importance of fame and image showed no significant relationship with SWB. On the other hand, the relative importance of money was negatively correlated to SWB. The comparable coefficients in the regression results were in line with correlation data. Among three physical-self domains, two (safety and hedonism) showed negative or no contribution while one (health) had a positive contribution to SWB.

H6 proposed that a positive relationship exists between household income and SWB. The evidence was mixed for this hypothesis. The study confirmed the positive relationship between income level and SWB in general. However, we divided the sample into two groups (high and low-income earners) and tested the impact of income above the median; we determined that low-income earners have relatively higher life satisfaction, holding everything else constant. Thus, we can conclude that making more money is important, but thinking about money more is detrimental to SWB, as suggested by H7.

Conclusion

Previous research has shown consistent evidence regarding the association between different aspirations and SWB. low SWB has clearly been linked to extrinsic values and high SWB to intrinsic values. However, most of those studies were conducted in Western countries or nations with Western values, leaving two important questions unanswered. First, are they applicable to countries with a significantly different culture? Second, are any aspiration domains missing in the existing studies?

Our study attempted to answer both questions. First, the purpose of the study was to test AI with extended domains in a cosmopolitan city with a mixed culture of materialist and spiritual values. Turkey in general—and Istanbul in particular—provides a unique opportunity to study the effect of different values. Turkish culture combines a mix of Western modernization undertaken in varying degrees since the 17th century with a strong desire to maintain traditional and religious values. Thus, the city provides a great opportunity for an almost natural social experiment to explore the relationship between different aspirations and SWB. The results confirmed the previous cross-cultural studies (Ryan et al.

1999) in terms of the positive relationship between intrinsic values and SWB. They were also consistent with the prediction of self-determination theory: as people give more importance to extrinsic values, they have less time to fulfill their psychological needs of autonomy, competence, and relatedness. As a result, people with materialist values end up having lower SWB.

PART III
FAILURE IN FINDING HAPPINESS IN TWO DIMENSIONS

Chapter 11

American Dream or Nightmare?

"For many, the American dream has become a nightmare."
—**Bernie Sanders**, U.S. Senator

Introduction

The American Dream is a national motto for Americans. It represents a set of ideals for everyone to prosper. John Adams, a founding father of the United States, defined the American Dream as "life should be better and richer and fuller for everyone, with opportunity for each according to ability or achievement" regardless of social class or circumstances of birth. Indeed, the American Dream is engraved in the Declaration of Independence, which announces that "all men are created equal" with the right to "life, liberty and the pursuit of happiness." Millions of people around the world embark on a quest for the same dream by immigrating to the United States.

I shall confess that I once had the same dream. After a long and challenging journey, I stepped on the dreamland in January 1999. It was truly a dream-like experience. I was amazed by the freedom, justice, productivity, and diversity of the American culture and system. I felt compelled to share my experience with the deprived people in my country. I wrote op-ed articles and participated in radio and TV shows to share my experience. I was echoing what Tocqueville had said about America almost two centuries ago: "Imagine, my dear friend, if you can, a society composed of all the nations of the world: English, French, Germans ..., everyone having a language, a belief, opinions that are different; in a word, a society without common prejudices, sentiments, ideas, without a national character, a hundred times happier than ours."[10]

My first impression did not last long. The more I learned about the culture, the more I become aware of its dark side. In this chapter, I will try to explore the data to see how the American dream becomes a nightmare for many Americans.

Happiness Crisis

It was Easterlin (1974) who first came up with some quantitative signs of the happiness crisis in capitalism. In his study covering the years 1946-1970, he found that despite a great increase in the real income per capita, there was no significant change in subjective well-being. He later completed a similar study for Japan and found that the average self-reported happiness level did not increase in Japan between 1958 and 1987 despite a fivefold increase in real income. Since that study, we have seen a surge in studies on happiness and income. Most of them confirm Easterlin's findings regarding the impact of monetary wealth on happiness. For instance, a Chinese study showed that the case is not entirely different in China, which has been experimenting with consumer culture for the last two decades. The study found remarkable economic growth from 1994 to 2005, with an increase of 250 percent in real income per capita, ownership of color television sets rising from 40 percent of households to 82 percent, and the number of people with a telephone jumping from 10 percent to 63 percent. Yet, this did not translate

---

10   From a letter sent on 9 June 1831 to a friend. Tocqueville copied this passage into his alphabetic notebook.

into higher life satisfaction. Instead, the percentage of people who said they were dissatisfied increased, and the percentage who said they were satisfied decreased (Kahneman & Krueger, 2006).

The Easterlin Paradox claims a lack of a direct correlation between average life satisfaction and income per capita across nations. In other words, even though rich people report higher life satisfaction than the poor in a given country, wealth does not explain differences in self-reported life satisfaction across countries or even in the same country over time. For instance, Frey (2008) found that income per capita jumped in Japan by a factor of 6 between 1958 and 1990, while average life satisfaction remained unchanged at a level of 2.7 on a four-point scale. Layard showed that "for countries above $20,000 a head, additional income is not associated with extra happiness" (Layard, 2005, p.33).

Despite some evidence of its failure in providing happiness (Diener, Suh, & Oishi, 1997; Easterbrook, 2003; Hamilton & Denniss, 2006; Kasser, 2002; Lane, 2000), the globalization of consumer culture and materialistic values is rapidly displacing traditional values. Indeed, those questionable new values are spreading all over the world. They have entered every realm of human life, including even religious places like churches, synagogues, and mosques. They have turned a human being into a consumption machine. But not only does a consumer culture fail to bring happiness, it also fails to protect the environment. It has produced many environmental problems, including unchecked growth in the production of solid waste and greenhouse gas emissions. Therefore, it is not sustainable in the long run (Aydin, 2010).

It is not just the weapons of mass destruction; it is also the products of mass consumption that are threatening the future of all living beings on this planet. With more and more consumption, people are no more, and sometimes even less, happy. This is neither desirable nor sustainable. In short, wealthy capitalist nations are currently experiencing a serious "happiness crisis" that is spreading around the world with the globalization of capitalism. Many studies have presented evidence for the existence of the happiness crisis without delving into its root causes (Lane, 2000).

More Money, but less happiness

As shown in the chart below, in the last four decades, the real income per capita for Americans has doubled. This means that on average they have improved their economic well-being by 100% compared to what they had in 1973. Since real income per capita disregards changes due to inflation, this improvement is real in an economic sense. Ironically, economic well-being made no difference in subjective well-being. Indeed, the percent of very happy people declined from 37 in 1973 to 33 in 2014. This is clear evidence that realizing the American dream in terms of economic wellbeing does not necessarily mean higher happiness. Indeed, it might mean a nightmare if we look at other indicators.

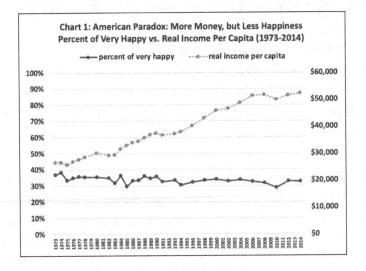

Data source: 1) real income per capita: U.S. Bureau of Economic Analysis, retrieved from FRED, Federal Reserve Bank of St. Louis; https://fred.stlouisfed.org/series/A939RX0Q048SBEA, October 26, 2018. 2) Happiness: General Social Survey: Trends in Psychological Well-Being, 1972-2014, NORC at the University of Chicago

Destruction of Faith

Since the Enlightenment, religions have lost ground against secularization. This is also true for the historically religious American society. It is important to note the difference between the United States and Europe in terms of their understanding of religious freedom. For Americans, historically, it means freedom for the religion while for Europeans, it means freedom from religion. Despite this fact, the data clearly shows that Americans are running away from religion. As shown in chart 2, the percent of those who identify themselves as Protestants dropped from 70% to 38% in four decades. During the same time period, there were almost no atheists in 1961 while in 2017, 20% of Americans define themselves as atheists.

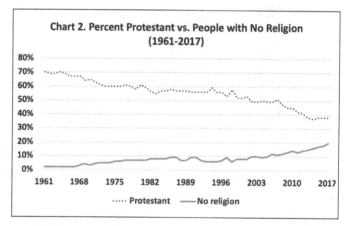

Source: Gallup survey, http://www.gallup.com/poll/1690/religion.aspx

Chart 3 shows the percent of atheist and agnostic people in major European countries. In the Czech Republic and the Netherlands, atheists account for half or more than half of the population. France is on the fast track to join this atheist club. UK, Germany, Spain, and Denmark are lagging by several percentage points. It is evident that before 2050, the European Union will lose its title of being a Christian Club. It will become an Atheist Club. Giving the increasing rate of atheism, it is not going to take long for even the United States to catch up with Europe by having an atheist majority society.

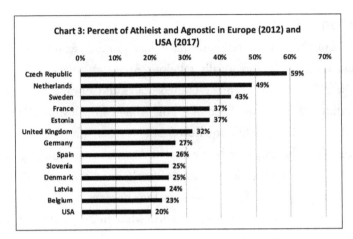

Source: Data for EU countries are from Eurobarometer Survey 2012. The data for USA is from Gallup Survey.

Destruction of Family

Plato in *The Republic* suggested abolishment of the family for the guardian class. He proposed a communal life: "All these women shall be wives in common to all the men, and not one of them shall live privately with any man; the children too should be held in common so that no parent shall know which is his own offspring, and no child shall know his parent." It seems that he believed in eugenics through communal life: "The best men must cohabit with the best women as many cases as possible and the worst with the worst in the fewest, and the offspring of the one must be reared and that of the other not, if the flock is to be as perfect as possible." He even suggested how to get rid of the inferiors: "The offspring of the inferior, and any of those of the other sort who are born defective, they will properly dispose of in secret, so that no one will know what has become of them. That is the condition of preserving the purity of the guardians' breed."[11]

It seems that Plato's utopic dream is going to be real in modern societies. Indeed, family as an institution is under an existential threat in the United States and Europe. For those who pursue happiness through hedonic pleasure, the family seems nothing but a burden. Even though for Americans, the family is an

---

11   The excerpt is available on the following website: http://www.worldfuturefund.org/wffmaster/ Reading/Quotes/plato.htm, accessed on October 26, 2018.

important religious and cultural institution, it appears they are moving toward a society without a traditional family. As seen in Chart 4, only one out of two adult individuals are married while one-third of adults never get married. Nearly one out five people are either divorced, separated, or widowed.

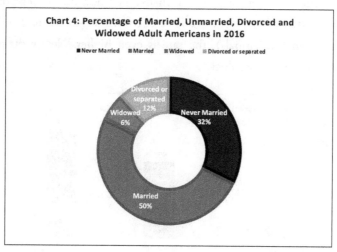

Source: 2017 Census https://www.census.gov/newsroom/ facts-for-features/2017/single-americans-week.html

Even though the percent of married people has been in decline in the last four decades, it seems that those who do get married have difficulty in sustaining it. As seen in Chart 5, nearly half of marriage ends up with divorce. Since the

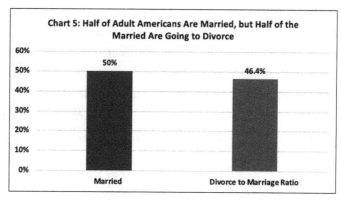

Source: https://www.cdc.gov/nchs/data/dvs/ national_marriage_divorce_rates_00-16.pdf

percentage of married includes those who re-marry as well, it is likely that only ten or fifteen percent of adult Americans have a life-long lasting marriage.

The family is a particularly important institution for raising a new generation. Today, for the majority of children, a traditional family of two parents is no longer an option. As seen in Chart 6, in five decades, the percent of children born out of wedlock has reached 40 percent from 7 percent in 1964. For the young generation (millennials), the rate is even higher. Nearly 60 percent of children are born out of wedlock.

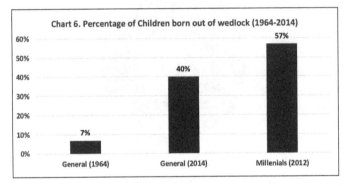

Source: 1) General: OECD 2) Millennials: Johns Hopkins study in 2012: http:// krieger.jhu.edu/sociology/wp-content/uploads/sites/28/2012/02/Read-Online.pdf

For most OECD countries, the percent of births out of wedlock is above 40. Chile and Costa Rica have 70 percent of births out of wedlock while several European countries have a rate above 50 percent. For the majority of countries, it may soon be the norm to have births of out of wedlock.

The regular surveys by the Pew Research Center reveal a significant social change regarding the number of children living with an unmarried parent. As seen in Chart 8, in 1968, 85 percent of children under 18 used to live with married parents but in 2017, only 65 percent of them lived with married parents. Thus, about one-third of American children are currently living with an unmarried parent.

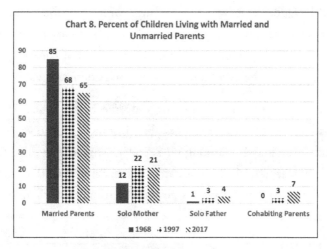

Data Source: Pew Research Center.

Destruction of Body and Soul

In developed countries, the increasing consumer culture seems to devour the human body and soul. Just two centuries ago, economist Thomas Malthus predicted that humanity would not have enough food for everyone; he argued that the population would multiply geometrically, but food would increase arithmetically. Even though we have many people starving in modern times, this is mainly due to a distribution problem, not a production problem. Generally

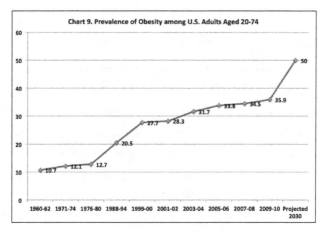

Source: NHANES data from the website:
www.cdc.gov/nhs/data/hestat/oesity_adult_09_10.html#table1

speaking, at the global level, we have no danger of facing a food shortage now or in the future. Ironically, we are facing an increasing risk of dying due to excessive food, as shown in the chart below. Currently, one-third of Americans are obese, and it is projected that by 2030, one of every two Americans will be obese.

Consumer culture is not destroying only the body; it also kills the soul through many psychological disorders. For instance, as shown in the chart below, a study on narcissism among U. S. college students revealed that college students are increasingly showing a narcissist character. For that matter, many thinks that Trump's victory provides powerful testimony to the moral decay of American society.

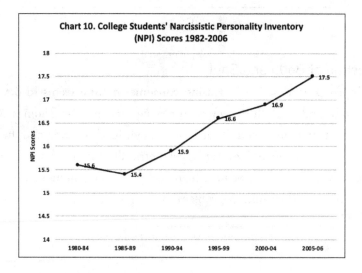

Public trust seems to be a growing problem. Pew Research Center has measured public trust since 1958. The percentage of people who agree with the following statement is at all-time low: "Most people can be trusted". In the 2014 survey, only one-third of people agreed that most people can be trusted.

As trust and family ties erode, more people prefer to live alone. In the United States, one-fourth of households have only one occupant. For some European countries, the rate goes up to 47%. If we look at the historical data since 1850, it is quite apparent that society at large is moving toward individualism. Particularly, retirees have a growing rate of moving toward a lonely life experience at a time when they might need more support[12].

Due to the weak social network, people are likely to be homeless if they become unemployed. Despite the economic boom, in 2017, more than half a million people were homeless. Over 1.1 million people are HIV infected. They have to rely on medicine for a lifetime.

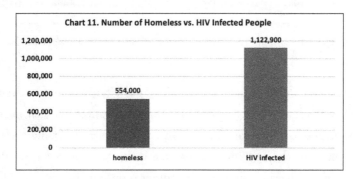

*Source: 1) homeless: 2017 data http://thedataface.
com/2018/01/public-health/american-homelessness; 2) HIV:
2015 data from Centers for Disease Controls and Prevention,
https://www.cdc.gov/hiv/statistics/overview/ataglance.html*

Stress and depression are two major psychological problems in modern societies. While a certain level of stress is not a problem, the data indicate that the stress level of people in developed countries is way above the healthy level. For instance, in the United States, the American Psychological Association conducts a periodic survey to measure stress levels among different groups. A healthy stress level is defined as 3.7 out of 10 in this measurement. As seen in the chart below, the new generation, in particular, is experiencing unusually high stress.

---

12   For further info, please refers to the following NY Times article: https://archive.nytimes.com/
      www.nytimes.com/imagepages/2012/02/05/sunday-review/05alone2.html

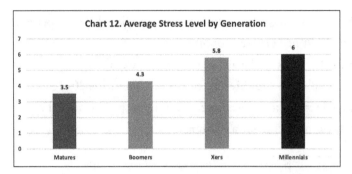

Source: 2015 Stress in America Survey by the American Psychological Association

It seems that the destruction of faith, family, body, and soul lead to the damage of individuals psychologically through depression. As seen in the chart below, one-fifth of adult females in the United States have had a major depressive episode. Ironically, the rate increased as the country recovered from the 2008 financial crisis and began experiencing another economic boom.

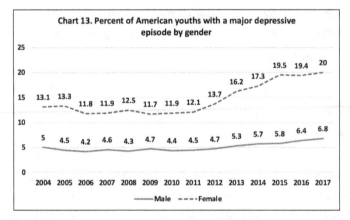

Source: 2017 National Survey on Drug Use and Health:
Detailed Tables, page 2818, available on www.statistica.com

An increasing number of people are using drugs and alcohol to suppress their psychological problems and diminishing life satisfaction. Although many people claim that they just use alcohol for having fun and socializing, the data indicate that at least one-third of people become alcoholic as shown below. Likewise, one of every two Americans has used marijuana, according to the 2017 Yahoo and Marist Poll. At least 16 percent of illicit drug users end up using a very addictive drug such as cocaine.

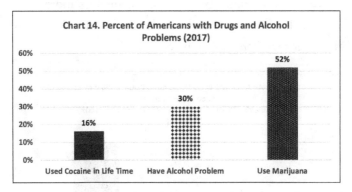

Source: 1) Cocaine: 2009 data from National Institute of Drug Abuse: https://www.drugabuse.gov/news-events/nida-notes/2009/11/united-states-ranks-first-in-lifetime-use-three-drugs; 2) Alcohol: https://www.businessinsider.com/nearly-30-percent-of-americans-are-alcoholics-2015-6 3) Marijuana: 2017 Yahoo and Marist Poll: https://www.nbcnews.com/news/us-news/new-poll-finds-majority-americans-have-smoked-pot-n747476

Indeed, Gallup surveys since 1969 reveal that the percentage of Americans who have tried marijuana is at an all-time high. Within five decades, usage has increased more than eleven-fold. What an even more alarming issue with marijuana is the starting age. Many people try marijuana when they are mentally mature enough to make a thoughtful decision. As of 2015, 7% of students in the eighth grade, 18% of those in the tenth grade, and 23% of those in the twelfth grade reported using marijuana in the last thirty days when the survey was conducted.

Destruction of Life

We argue that unless the social and psychological problems discussed above are appropriately addressed, they lead to the destruction of life for many people. Thus, it is essential to examine the lives lost due to homicide, suicide, and drug overdose.

The chart below is based on the most recent data on homicide and suicide per 100K people in a year. Even though many people look at crime rates when they search for renting or buying a house because they do not want to be killed by others, perhaps they should be afraid of themselves more than of others. Indeed, the chart clearly shows that for an American, the odds of killing oneself is 2.5 times greater than being killed by others.

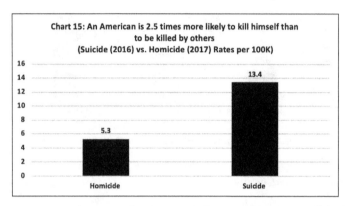

Data source: 1) Homicide: FBI Data for 2017, https://ucr.fbi.gov/ crime-in-the-u.s/2017/crime-in-the-u.s.-2017/topic-pages/tables/ table-1; 2) Suicide: 2016 data from American Foundation for Suicide Prevention: https://afsp.org/about-suicide/suicide-statistics/

Illicit drugs pose an even greater threat to human life compared to homicide and suicide. Indeed, in 2017, 72,000 people lost their lives due to a drug overdose. Using the same metric of calculating death per 100K, as shown in the chart below, it seems that an American is four times more likely to kill himself by drug overdose than to be killed by others. Since in reality, death from drug overdose is a form of suicide, even if unintentional, we shall combine the deaths from suicide and drugs. In this case, if you live in the United States, you are SEVEN times more likely to kill yourself than to be killed by others.

We think the number of people killed due to preventable homicide, suicide, and drug overdose should be taken very seriously. Indeed, it is alarming that the malaise of modernity produces casualties greater than many terrible wars. To put it into perspective, we provide the number of people killed during the

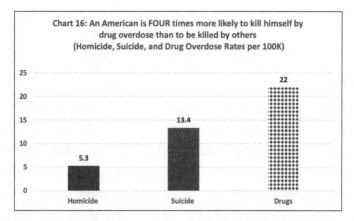

Data source: Homicide and suicide data are from the same source in the previous chart. Drugs Overdose: 2017 data from National Institute of Drug Abuse: https://www.drugabuse.gov/related-topics/trends-statistics/overdose-death-rates

American war against homicide, suicide, and drug overdose and the number of people killed in the Syrian Civil War in the last eight years. Since what is killing Americans is ultimately moral issues, we call it the "American Moral War." We used the highest estimate of human casualties for the "Syrian Civil War." Despite

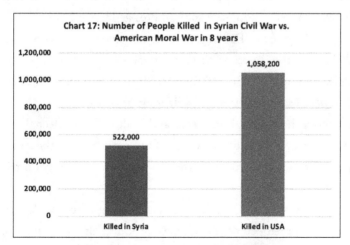

Source: Syrian Civil War: The highest estimate by activist groups as reported in Wikipedia, accessed on October 23, 2018. American Moral War: Calculated based on the actual data in the previous chart.

this, we found the number of Americans killed in the moral war was twice the number of those who died in the Syrian civil war.

Conclusion

We think that the data discussed in this chapter clearly point to the American Nightmare rather than the American Dream. Even though most Americans ran away from Europe to live their religion freely, the data show that they are increasingly running away from their religion as they pursue materialistic aspirations. Free market capitalism has helped the majority to realize their dream of having a big house, big car, and big fun. However, the system failed to fulfill its promise of increasing happiness. The high materialism comes with a trade-off: major destruction in faith, family, body, soul, and life. In other words, the search for hedonic happiness through consumer culture results in disappointment, depression, and destruction.

In fact, an ongoing longitudinal study on happiness and health by the Harvard Study of Adult Development provides compelling answers for the failure of the American Dream. The study is considered one of the world's longest studies of adult life, having started in 1938 during the Great Depression. The study divided the participants into two groups based on their education and income. The first group was chosen among the sophomores at Harvard College; the second was a group of boys from Boston's poorest neighborhoods who were selected specifically because they were from some of the most troubled and disadvantaged families in Boston in the 1930s. In the past 79 years, the researchers tracked the lives of 724 people in both groups, following up with each one on an annual basis to ask about their work, home lives, and health. They collected information through both survey and medical records of the participants. The study revealed that happy and healthy people were those who maintained a good relationship with family, friends, and community.

As discussed above, the data reveal that, through free market capitalism, we, the people of developed countries, have produced and consumed more, but enjoyed less. We have multiplied our material possessions but lost our spiritual dimensions. We have learned how to make a great living but forgotten how to live a great life. We have built bigger houses but destroyed bigger families. We have gained more knowledge but are left with less truth. We have discovered the far edges of the outer universe but dismissed the nearest inner universe. We have found our way to the moon but lost our way to our neighbors. We have invented better communication tools but forgotten how to communicate with others. We have written better laws to protect our freedom from intruders but forgotten how to protect our freedom from animalistic and egotistic desires.

Chapter 12

Nietzsche's Last Man and Unhappy Nihilist

"He who has a why to live can bear almost any how."
—Friedrich Nietzsche

Introduction

Nietzsche was a great philosopher who foresaw the malaise of modern life in pursuit of pleasure. He sharply criticized the hedonic consumer culture in terms of making pleasure the end of human life. He believed that humans had a high potential to reach excellence, which he called Ubermensch (sometimes it is translated as superman. Perhaps, it is better to call it "virtuous/ accomplished man"): "Man is a rope stretched between the animal and the Ubermensch— a rope over an abyss" (Nietzsche 2007, 11). If the human did not realize his potential through certain virtue, he was doomed to stay as an animal. Nietzsche's grand project was the revaluation of existing values. It was giving a new meaning to life. For him, this was not merely an intellectual interest. It was dear to his own life as he went through a total transformation when he became dissatisfied with his life. Indeed, he considered it his mission to bring real meaning to human life: "I want to teach men the sense of their existence: the Ubermensch, the lighting out of the dark cloud of man" (p. 16). He urged readers to make the Ubermensch be the meaning of the earth.

Fall of humanity

Nietzsche was well aware of the fall of human beings. He was disgusted with modern life and spent the last decade of his life in isolation. As he declared the death of God in the life of people, he also declared the death of humanity. He argues that "last man" of modern society "has no aspiration but pitiable comfort." In other words, the last man is decadent, pursuing small pleasures. He does not know "love, knowledge, and reality" (Nietzsche, 2007, 13). He is like a pleasure-seeking machine wounded by happiness. He pursues "poisonous little pleasure." "A little poison now and then: that makes pleasant dreams. And much poison at last for a pleasant death" (p. 14). His life is without any meaning (p. 16). Everything in his life, "All is empty, all is alike, and all have been" (p. 116). He is selfish and cannot go beyond praise and blame (p. 67). He only loves himself (p. 54). Even his love of the neighbor is "bad love" of himself. He is narcissist and egoist. "Men who are nothing more than a big eye or a big mouth or a big belly or something else big—I call such people inverse cripples" (p. 120). Men are shattered by modern life. "This is the terrible thing to my eye that I find man broken up, and scattered about, as on a battle- and butcher- ground. And when my eye flees from the present to the past, it always finds the same: fragments and limbs and fearful chances- but no men!" (p. 121).

Nietzsche could not believe how modern people could think of small pleasure as a worthy aspiration in life. He wept for the fall of humanity. He escaped to seclusion to protect himself and prescribed a solution for his fellow beings. He defined his essential goal as "to compose" fragmented modern men "into one and gather together what is fragmented and riddle and fearful chance" (p. 121). He thought that humans had great potential to accomplish great things in life. He named his ideal "Übermensch." Nietzsche's Superman should not be confused with Hollywood's Superman. Nietzsche's Übermensch had higher aspirations and a great mission in life. Übermensch does not live for small pleasure. He wants to live for "the sake of his virtue, he wants to live on and to live no more… (his soul) is extravagant, who wants no thanks and returns none… (his) Soul is deep, even in being wounded." (p. 12). He tells himself that "I must perfect myself, therefore, I now avoid my happiness and present myself to every unhappiness" (p. 139). To be Ubermensch, he shall "build over and beyond" himself… he must be "the self-conqueror, the ruler of (his) senses, the master of (his) virtues" (p. 61).

Seeking small pleasure in the city

Nietzsche defined the modern city in which we "have nothing to seek and everything to lose" (p. 160). He cried that "everything of today. it is falling, it is decaying." (p. 179). He found it disgusting that people pursued "the eternal recurrence of the smallest" (p. 188). He thought that people were fragmented in modern life (p. 120). "The world never sank so deep" (p. 211). It had lost its magic. "There is much filth in the world" (p.175). Modern humans seek small happiness in this world "by converting to cows" (p. 230). Heaven on earth is only possible through this conversion: "Unless we are converted and become as cows, we shall not enter into the kingdom of heaven" (p. 230). He even further argued that we are more "apes than apes." In other words, we make the animal pleasure center to our lives even more than an animal. He saw value in such a life. "He who has always overindulged himself is at sickened by his overindulgence" (p.132). He urged to "spit on the great city that is the great trash heap where all the scum froths together! Spit on the city of compressed souls and narrow chests, of slit eyes and sticky fingers—on the city of the importunate, the shameless, the scribble- and scream-throats, the overheated ambitious ones: where everything infirm, infamous, lustful, gloomy, insipid, ulcerous, and conspiratorial festers together. Spit on the great city and turn back!" (p.152)

Metamorphosis of camel, lion, and child

Nietzsche argued that "many die too late and a few die too early" (Nietzsche 2007, 63). He envisioned the rise of Übermensch through three metamorphoses (p.25). First, Übermensch has to turn into a camel kneeling in front of the challenges in life in order to excel in virtue. This is "to humiliate oneself to mortify one's pride… to feed on the acorns and grass of knowledge, and for the sake of truth to the hunger of soul…" (p.25). Second, Übermensch has to transform into a lion to overcome his ego, to go beyond self. "Always the self listens and seeks; it compares, masters, conquers, and destroys. It rules and is in control of the "I" too. Behind your thoughts and feelings, my brother, there is a mighty lord, an unknown sage his name is self." (p.32). By being a lion, he "would conquer his freedom and be master in his own desert. (p.25). Third, Übermensch should be a child living like a newborn to reality and virtue. "The child is innocence and forgetting, a new beginning. (p.26) Thus, he could aim for eternity, the one whom Nietzsche truly loved: "Never did I find the woman by whom I wanted children, unless it be this woman whom I love: for I love you, O eternity! for I love you, O eternity! (p.197) Übermensch will live life for the sake of truth, virtue, and reality without fear of being blamed or desire of being praised.

Figure 1. Metaphorical Transformation of Human

Modern man and marketplace

Nietzsche believes that modern man is surrounded by a marketplace full of poisonous flies. He has to run to solitude to preserve his life. "Where solitude ends, there the marketplace begins; and where the marketplace begins, there also begins the noise of the great actors and buzzing of the poisonous flies" (p.46). These flies of the marketplace "want blood from you in all innocence, their bloodless souls crave blood- and therefore they sting in all innocence" (p.47). "They buzz around you even with their praise and their praise is importunity. They want to be close to your skin and your blood" (p.48). The solution is to escape to solitude: "Flee, my friend, into your solitude: I see you stung all over by the poisonous flies…. Flee into your solitude! You have lived too closely to the small and the pitiable. Flee from their invisible vengeance! Towards you, they have nothing but vengeance" (p.47).

Nihilism: infinite nothing

Nietzsche named the value crisis of modern man as nihilism. He perceived nihilism as a widespread phenomenon that could be seen as the root of many social problems. Even though he discussed the problem of nihilism in many of his writings, he gave explicit warning in his notebooks, which were published posthumously (Nietzsche & Handwerk, 2013). Nietzsche portrayed nihilism as emptying the world and human life from any meaning, purpose, morality, and essential value.

In his notebooks, Nietzsche referred to the death of Christianity as the beginning of nihilism. In his view, Christianity was the source of intrinsic value and morality in the West. It was also a source of objective knowledge and truth. In other words, people used to believe in the existence of God as real and Christianity as authentic knowledge from God. They would live their lives within Christian ideals trying to fulfill their God-given mission. Ironically, it was the drive for the truth that eventually led to the death of God and the removal of Christianity from the hearts of people.

In his famous aphorism of the madman in *The Gay Science*, Nietzsche declared the death of God at hand of a human. He was literally telling Christian establishments that they could not deceive us by their conflicting concepts of God and contradiction of religious edicts. As rational modern men, we could not accept such baloney beliefs. Thus, if there is no God, there is no room for God-centered morality and meaning. Nietzsche was aware of the cost of killing God. For him, the death of God was like the death of the Sun for the earth. It was the fall to darkness. It was the fall to infinite nothing:

"But how did we do this? How could we drink up the sea? Who gave us the sponge to wipe away the entire horizon? What were we doing when we unchained this earth from its sun? Whither is it moving now? Whither are we moving? Away from all suns? Are we not plunging continually? Backward,

sideward, forward, in all directions? Is there still any up or down? Are we not straying, as through an infinite nothing? Do we not feel the breath of empty space? Has it not become colder? Is not night continually closing in on us? Do we not need to light lanterns in the morning?"(F. W. Nietzsche, Kaufmann, & Kaufmann, 1974)

With the death of God, Nietzsche was warning humanity for the problem of nihilism as one of the greatest problems ever: "I praise, I do not reproach, [nihilism's] arrival. I believe it is one of the greatest crises, a moment of the deepest self-reflection of humanity. Whether man recovers from it, whether he becomes master of this crisis, is a question of his strength!" (Levy, 1923)

Nietzsche defines nihilist person as follows: "A nihilist is a man who judges of the world as it is that it ought not to be, and of the world as it ought to be that it does not exist. According to this view, our existence (action, suffering, willing, feeling) has no meaning: the pathos of 'in vain' is the nihilists' pathos — at the same time, as pathos, an inconsistency on the part of the nihilists." (F. W. Nietzsche & Handwerk, 2013).

Will to Power

For Nietzsche, the meaning was not something to be discovered. Rather, it is something to be built. Even though everything might seem ultimately meaningless, one with a strong will could build meaning for oneself. Otherwise, life is not endurable:

"It is a measure of the degree of strength of will to what extent one can do without meaning in things, to what extent one can endure to live in a meaningless world because one organizes a small portion of it oneself." (Nietzsche, 2012, *The Will to Power*)

Nietzsche went into detail explaining the governing force behind mysterious material transformation through the will to power. He described this world as it appeared in his mirror:

"And do you know what "the world" is to me? Shall I show it to you in my mirror? This world: a monster of energy, without beginning, without end; a firm, iron magnitude of force that does not grow bigger or smaller, that does not expend itself but only transforms itself; as a whole, of unalterable size, a household without expenses or losses, but likewise without increase or income; enclosed by "nothingness" as by a boundary; not something blurry or wasted, not something endlessly extended, but set in a definite space as a definite force, and not a space that might be "empty" here or there, but rather as force throughout, as a play of forces and waves of forces, at the same time one and many, increasing here and at the same time decreasing there; a sea of forces flowing and rushing together, eternally changing, eternally flooding back, with tremendous years of recurrence, with an ebb and a flood of its forms; …This world is the will to power—and nothing besides! And you yourselves are also this will to power—and nothing besides!" (Nietzsche, 2012, pt. 1067).

Conclusion

In short, nihilism can be defined as the devaluation of the highest values. It is the devaluation of sacred texts. It is a devaluation of morality. It is a devaluation of a human being. According to Nietzsche, the principal motive behind this devaluation was the Will to Power. Ironically, the Will to Power was also the principle of every earlier valuation of values (Müller Lauter, 1999, p.268). Nietzsche's nihilism might help us to understand the intrinsic motive behind conspicuous consumption. We can talk about "commodity nihilism" with two different meaning. First, it means to consume for the sake of consumption (or small pleasure) without considering any higher goals such as aesthetic or humanistic values. It is like pursuing "pitiable comfort" aiming to make money and consume without having any goal of innate growth. Second, "commodity nihilism" means consuming to close the gap of the lost inherent value of being a human being. It is value seeking by those who think they do not have any intrinsic value anymore. It is an attempt to substitute extrinsic value with intrinsic one. It is an effort to fill the abyss left by the death of religion in the West.

We think Neitzsche's three metaphors might help us to understand the dimensional transformation in our search for happiness. At the hedonic dimension, we resemble a camel submitting to our desires for the sake of pleasure. Due to the law of diminishing marginal utility, we will eventually find no satisfaction in pursuing pleasure. As we gain wisdom and courage, we will move to the eudemonic dimension fighting against our conflicting desires. We will be like a lion in the wilderness of worldly life. We will gain freedom from meaningless desires to follow the mind for a meaningful life. However, we will reach a dead end at this dimension as well. As we age, we could not avoid exploring the ultimate meaning of life and asking some existentional questions. That is when we will be seeking life satisfaction at the G-donic dimension through spirituality.

Chapter 13

Searching for Happiness while Sinking into Depression

"Experience had taught me that all the things which regularly occur in ordinary life are empty and futile"
—Spinoza

Introduction

Over two thousand years ago, Socrates challenged a human being to examine his/her life. He claimed that "an unexamined life is not worth living." Schopenhauer was a very deep thinker in the 1800s. After carefully examining his life, he claimed that life was not worth living. This message seems to resonate with an increasing number of people who commit suicide. Even more people attempt to commit suicide, and many come very close to it. Why? Schopenhauer thought that we were asking the wrong question. From his perspective, we should not ask why people commit suicide. Rather, we should ask why they do not commit suicide. In other words, it is normal to commit suicide. It is abnormal not to commit suicide, once we realize that life is not worth living. In this chapter, I will explore the causes of the mid-life crisis.

We argue that a complete happiness equation consists of three terms: a hedonic utility term, an additive meaning term, and a multiplicative term. It is possible to ignore the meaning term and multiplicative terms by pursuing hedonic happiness. Indeed, that is what many young and healthy people do. Adding a meaning term would potentially increase total utility and the level of happiness. As discussed before, seeking happiness through meaning or flourishing is eudemonic happiness, as originally suggested by Aristotle. This will bring a higher level of satisfaction. Thus, one could be happy with the first and second terms for a while. Eventually, one will begin to reflect on the F (faith) multiplier, which is about the transcendental meaning of everything. If that is found to be zero, then, everything will ultimately become meaningless as shown below:

$$H_{el} = \{U\ (H, D, B, L) + M\ (H, D, B, L)\} * F = 0 \text{ if } F = 0$$

We argue that those who seek happiness by having, doing, being, and meaning might reach a dead end and find happiness with none. They do not experience happiness even if they have everything. For them, nothing could bring lasting happiness. Therefore, life is doomed to end in misery rather than happiness.

Figure 1. Happiness Loop with Nothing

Midlife Crisis and Incomplete Happiness Equation

Why does one face a happiness crisis in mid-life? We do not think it is just a coincidence that people often face a mid-life crisis in their 40s. It can be attributed to many reasons.

First, in a consumer society, we are constantly told that happiness is the function of what we have, do, and are in life. Given the fact that as we grow, we see many people follow this happiness path, we are likely to do so, too.

Second, at a young age, we are capable of experiencing higher hedonic pleasure if we are healthy and wealthy.

Third, given our curious nature, we want to experience many things just to know what they are like.

Fourth, by our mid-life, we have enough experience to learn that diminishing marginal utility and adaptation bring down our pleasure of having, doing, and being to a very low level.

Fifth, as we get older, we will realize that life is not just fun. We see many adversities and calamities which cause significant pain. We are likely to have a serios illness. We begin experiencing weakness in our body. This will remind us of the downside of life.

Sixth, we will see the death of known and beloved people. We will know that we cannot escape from the painful end of death. As a result, we begin asking existential questions. If we do not find any satisfying answers to them, we will realize that everything is ultimately meaningless. Therefore, it will be hard to find an excuse to live longer. We either have to indulge in something to forget our ultimate fate, or we need to seek a different path that might lead to the answers to existential questions. In other words, we will either seek help from alcohol, drugs, or other addictive mind-blocking means to forget troubling questions, or, we will pursue a spiritual path to explore answers to our questions.

Ironically, it is our very success that leads us to the ultimate failure. The more we succeed with having, doing, and being in life, the more likely we are to face a mid-life crisis. Failing or struggling individuals might not find time to examine life. They might die while still deprived of having, doing, and being. The successful ones would learn from their experiences that having, doing, being could not bring authentic happiness. They would know transient meaning would increase happiness, but not enough to bring lasting satisfaction.

We argue that it is more likely to fall into a mid-life crisis if we limit our pursuant of happiness to hedonic and even eudemonic happiness. In early life, we would experiment with having, doing, and being. We would hit the dead end through the DEAD loop of deprivation, emulation, achievement, and disappointment. Instead of learning our lesson, we repeat the cycles with different items, though the end result will be the same. As we get older, we are likely to seek happiness through meaning. However, as we make meaning the center of our lives, we could not help asking the ultimate meaning of everything in life. Our success in achieving having, doing, being, and worldly meaning might ultimately result in failure.

If we have no belief in an afterlife, it will become apparent to us that everything is ultimately meaningless. Though adding worldly meaning increases our marginal utility at an increasing rate for a while, it will eventually decrease toward zero. We will live in a two-dimensional flat world which is a shadow-like transient reality. It does not matter how much shadow we accumulate in our life, we will soon realize that it means nothing. Thus, the DEAD loop of our happiness search is likely to lead to depression as shown below:

Figure 2. DEAD Loop of Happiness and Depression

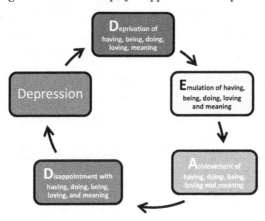

Tolstoy's Failure to Find Happiness

Leo Tolstoy (1828-1910) was a famous Russian novelist. His masterpieces *War and Peace* and *Anna Karenina* are considered some of the best historical fiction ever published. He provided an elegant account of his own mid-life crisis in the book, *A Confession*[13]. He was from a wealthy family and had a lot of material things from the beginning. He began seeking happiness by indulging in "doing" pleasant events. He also tried happiness through "being" as well through authorship. However, he later confessed that having, doing, and being brought him misery, not happiness. After a long internal fight, near the end of his life, he gave up his wealth and privilege and left his house to live among the peasants. He denounced his fame as a writer and regarded his literary work as worthless. As a wandering ascetic, he died in a train station two years after leaving his house.

Need and greed

Though Tolstoy was from an aristocratic family, he realized that the greedy nature of human beings could never be satisfied by having more and more. However, it was not about the need. It was about desire. He gave an example of a peasant who wished to be very rich. His wish was granted. He began adding more land to his property in the village. However, each time, he would get new land, he would desire even more. He became obsessed with more wealth. One day, he heard that some naïve people were living in a remote village. They would sell their properties at a very low price. He decided to go there to get more land. When he arrived, he was told that for a small amount, he could own as much land as he could walk on from sunrise to sunset. The only condition was that he had to make it to the starting point before sunset. He liked the deal and paid the money. At sunrise, he began walking across the vast land and leaving a mark on his pathway. He was extremely joyful as he thought how much land he would have by sunset. He even forgot to track the time. When he remembered that he had to go back, he was already too far from the starting point. He began running back. He ran and ran without relaxing. He felt as if the sun were running towards sunset faster than he was. He was very tired and despairing by the time he was about to reach the

---

13 The book is freely available on the Internet. The excerpts in this chapter are taken from the following website: http://www.online-literature.com/tolstoy/a-confession/, accessed on March 10, 2019.

starting point. He barely made it. He was filled with joy but collapsed from being too tired. He died on the spot and was buried there. Tolstoy concluded the story by saying that a greedy human being actually needs only a small piece of land as a grave. Everything else is nothing, a meaningless race to misery.

Shifting to eudemonic happiness

At the age of fifteen, Tolstoy realized that hedonic happiness could not bring satisfaction. He shifted toward eudemonic happiness by establishing a family and living a meaningful life through raising children. For a long time, his whole life was centered around his wife and children. Meanwhile, he was working hard for self-development. It paid off. He became a very successful literary writer worldwide.

For Tolstoy, his career success was the ultimate cause of failure for him. He confessed that in the early decades of his life, he was blind to the reality of the inevitable end of his success. He managed to earn international fame through writing. He also earned a good amount of money. What he was producing had temporal meaning in terms of enlightening others. However, he confessed that while he was guiding others, he realized that he did not know how to conduct himself: "how to teach others while myself knowing nothing."

He was in his fifties when he began experiencing a deep crisis. For him, the problem arose from asking existential questions such as "Who am I? Why do I live?" He did not ask those questions casually but realized that they were fundamental. He could not help but think about those questions, again and again. The question of meaning, "that which at the age of fifty brought me to the verge of suicide—was the simplest of questions, lying in the soul of every man from the foolish child to the wisest elder: it was a question without an answer to which one cannot live, as I had found by experience." (*A Confession*, Chapter 5)

He raised series of questions regarding the meaning of life: "But what does it matter to me? What of it? Why go on making any effort? How [do I] go on living? What will come of what I am doing today or shall do tomorrow? What will [be]come of my whole life? Why should I live, why wish for anything, or do anything? Is there any meaning in my life that the inevitable death awaiting me does not destroy? What am I, with my desires? Why do I live? What must I do? What is the meaning of my life? Why do I exist?" He told himself that "if these questions constantly repeated themselves they would have to be answered. And I tried to answer them. The questions seemed such stupid, simple, childish ones; but as soon as I touched them and tried to solve them I at once became convinced, first, that they are not childish and stupid but the most important and profound of life's questions" (*A Confession*, Chapter 3). For him, not having any answer to those existential questions made everything meaningless.

Dead end with eudemonic happiness

Tolstoy was not happy with temporal meaning, either. He would reflect on his great works and say to himself: "Very well; you will be more famous than Gogol or Pushkin or Shakespeare or Moliere, or than all the writers in the world—and what of it? And I could find no reply at all. The questions would not wait, they had to be answered at once, and if I did not answer them, it was impossible to live. But there was no answer" (*A Confession*, Chapter 3). In other words, everything including worldwide fame would eventually be "nothing." Tolstoy was intelligent enough to know that it is not worth working for ultimately nothing.

Tolstoy went through severe depression while dealing with those questions. He described his inner feeling as follows "I felt that what I had been standing on had collapsed and that I had nothing left under my feet. What I had lived on no longer existed, and there was nothing left…. My life came to a standstill. I could breathe, eat, drink, and sleep, and I could not help doing these things; but there was no life, for there were no wishes the fulfillment of which I could consider reasonable" (*A Confession*, Chapter 3).

For Tolstoy, it was mortality that made everything ultimately meaningless. He considered death as the ultimate destroyer of everything. If nothing can escape this destruction, then, why work on building anything. For him, the reality of death revealed the truth of life. "The truth was that life is meaningless. I had as it was lived, lived, and walked, walked, till I had come to a precipice and saw clearly that there was nothing ahead of me but destruction. It was impossible to stop, impossible to go back, and impossible to close my eyes or avoid seeing that there was nothing ahead but suffering and real death—complete annihilation" (*A Confession*, Chapter 3).

Life as a meaningless, stupid joke

Tolstoy was asking the "then, what?" question and finding nothing at the end. This is what Nietzsche would call "infinite nothing." It does not matter how much we succeed or gain in life, it all eventually turns to nothing. Thus, the maximum one can accomplish in life is "infinite nothing." For Tolstoy, it would be stupid to work for "infinite nothing." Indeed, when he was searching for meaning, he perceived his entire life as a "stupid joke": "My life is a stupid and spiteful joke someone has played on me. Though I did not acknowledge a "someone" who created me, yet such a presentation—that someone had played an evil and stupid joke on me by placing me in the world—was the form of expression that suggested itself most naturally to me" (*A Confession*, Chapter 4).

For Tolstoy, the joke was to see how we work hard to accumulate having, doing, and being while eventually realizing they are nothing: "Involuntarily it appeared to me that there, somewhere, was someone who amused himself by watching how I lived for thirty or forty years: learning, developing, maturing in body and mind, and how, having with matured mental powers reached the summit of life from which it all lay before me, I stood on that summit—like an archfool—seeing clearly that there is nothing in life, and that there has been and will be nothing. And *he* was amused."

As an atheist, Tolstoy at the time did not believe there was someone out there laughing at stupid human life. He said that "whether that 'someone' laughing at me existed or not, I was none the better off. I could give no reasonable meaning to any single action or my whole life. I was only surprised that I could have avoided understanding this from the very beginning—it has been so long known to all. Today or tomorrow sickness and death will come (they had come already) to those I love or to me; nothing will remain but stench and worms. Sooner or later my affairs, whatever they may be, will be forgotten, and I shall not exist" (*A Confession*, Chapter 4).

Life as a painful tragedy

Tolstoy was shocked at how many people failed to see the stupidity of life and still pursued pleasure: "How can man fail to see this? And how go on living? That is what is surprising! One can only live while one is intoxicated with life; as soon as one is sober it is impossible not to see that it is all a mere fraud and a stupid fraud! That is precisely what it is: there is nothing either amusing" (*A Confession*, Chapter 4). In other words, as long as we use our mind, we cannot avoid seeing the ultimate meaninglessness in everything. If so, how can we stick with life?

Tolstoy shared an old, but famous Eastern fable to illuminate how people still find pleasure in life. The story goes like this: a traveler on a long journey was going through a forest. While traveling on foot, he was chased by a furious beast. Running for his life, he ended up jumping into a dry well to avoid the beast. The well was quite deep. In the middle, he found a huge tree and clung to a branch of the tree. He looked at the bottom and saw a giant dragon that opened its jaws waiting to swallow him. Thus, he could go neither up and nor down. While trying to assess how safe the tree was, he noticed that the tree was attached to the wall of the well by two roots. Strangely, there were two rats, one white and one black, gnawing the roots. Thus, it was just a matter of time before he fell into the jaws of the waiting dragon. While left in such a miserable situation, the traveler noticed some drops of honey on the leaves of the tree. The traveler is left with the puzzling question of whether it is possible to enjoy the honey by denying the reality.

For Tolstoy, the fable above revealed the reality we all face. The dragon is death while the tree is life. White and black rats are day and night. Thus, we cannot avoid falling into the mouth of the dragon. Drops of honey are pleasant events in life. Tolstoy reflected on his life and found it difficult to enjoy his honey: "two drops of honey which diverted my eyes from the cruel truth longer than the rest: my love of family, and writing—art as I called it—were no longer sweet to me."

As a father of thirteen children, Tolstoy was an exceptionally dedicated parent. However, he found no reason to live for his loving wife and children. It was not that he did not care for his family. Actually, he cared too much to allow himself to think about their entire lives. He did not want to ignore the miserable reality for his family. "But my family—wife, and children—are also human. They are placed just as I am: they must either live in a lie or see a terrible truth. Why should they live? Why should I love them, guard them, bring them up, or watch them? That they may come to the despair that I feel, or else be stupid?" (*A*

Confession, Chapter 4) In other words, Tolstoy did not want to deceive himself. He did not want to deceive his family, either. Therefore, he did not want to play a game as if everything were OK. He saw the dragon was waiting for him and his family. Of course, it was a horrible situation. However, it was reality. Rationally, the best option was to kill yourself rather than waiting to be killed at any time by the dragon. For almost three years, Tolstoy seriously considered ending this torture: "The horror of darkness was too great, and I wished to free myself from it as quickly as possible by noose or bullet. That was the feeling which drew me most strongly towards suicide" (*A Confession*, Chapter 4).

Four types of people

Tolstoy put people into four categories based on their attitude toward life. The first group is ignorant, like the very young or those with low intelligence. They do not ask the question of life. "They see neither the dragon that awaits them nor the mice gnawing the shrub by which they are hanging, and they lick the drops of honey, but they lick those drops of honey only for a while: something will turn their attention to the dragon and the mice, and there will be an end to their liking" (*A Confession*, Chapter 7). Therefore, for Tolstoy, nothing could be learned from the ignorant. They would soon realize their misery. Thus, ignorance is bliss for a while. Sooner or later, they will wake up from the pleasant dream and face the horrible reality.

The second group of people is the pleasure-seeking hedonists. "while knowing the hopelessness of life, in making use meanwhile of the advantages one has, disregarding the dragon and the mice, and licking the honey in the best way, especially if there is much of it within reach.... because a man hath no better thing under the sun, than to eat, and to drink, and to be merry..." For Tolstoy, this path was not acceptable either. One has to be dull to ignore the dragon, mice, and the beast. "The dullness of these people's imagination enables them to forget the things that gave Buddha no peace—the inevitability of sickness, old age, and death, those who, to avoid seeing the question, lick the honey. I could not imitate these people; not having their dullness of imagination I could not artificially produce it in myself. I could not tear my eyes from the mice and the dragon, as no vital man can after he has once seen the truth of the situation and yet clinging to life, knowing in advance that nothing can come of it" (*A Confession*, Chapter 7).

The third group is courageous people who understand that everything is ultimately meaningless. They examine the life and realize it is not worth living. "Having understood that life is evil and stupid," they end it by committing suicide. For Tolstoy, those were the most courageous people, a group he aspired to be in.

The fourth group is those for whom life is meaningless, "and still go on living, washing oneself, dressing, dining, talking, and even writing books." Tolstoy put himself among this cowardly group. Though he acknowledged it was "repulsive and tormenting," he remained in this group. "People of this kind know that death is better than life, but not having the strength to act rationally—to end the deception quickly and kill themselves—they seem to wait for something." Tolstoy argued that everyone around him was in one of those four groups: "Looking at the narrow circle of my equals, I saw only people who had not understood the question, or who had understood it and drowned it in life's intoxication, or had understood it and ended their lives, or had understood it and yet from weakness were living out their desperate life. And I saw no others" (*A Confession*, Chapter 7).

Seeking the ultimate meaning

The only thing that kept Tolstoy alive was his hope of finding an answer to his existential questions. He did not just wait. He engaged in an active search. He knocked at the doors of philosophers, scientists, the religious establishment, and ordinary peasants. He asked science about the meaning of life. The answer he got was: "You are what you call your 'life'; you are a transitory, casual cohesion of particles. The mutual interactions and changes of these particles produce in you what you call your 'life.' That cohesion will last sometime; afterward, the interaction of these particles will cease and what you call 'life' will cease, and so will all your questions. You are an accidentally united little lump of something" (*A Confession*, Chapter 7) In other words, from a materialist scientific perspective, he realized that there is no ultimate meaning of life. We are nothing but an accidental product of some elements. We are like a wave of a large ocean with a short appearance. In Sartre's terms, life is nothing but "an unpleasant interruption to a peaceful nonexistence". For Tolstoy, science provided only instrumental knowledge. It provided no comfort because it did not have an answer to the meaning of life question. It only dealt with the finite. It connected finite with finite. It had no way to link finite to infinite.

Tolstoy posed the question of death as the ultimate destroyer to philosophers. Even though he found great attention to his question among philosophers, he failed to get an answer. "However, I may turn these replies of philosophy, I can never obtain anything like an answer—and not because, as in the clear experimental sphere, the reply does not relate to my question, but because here, though all the mental work is directed just to my question, there is no answer. Instead of an answer, one gets the same question, only in a complex form" (*A Confession*, Chapter 7). Therefore, philosophy did not bring him any relief. Rather, it increased his pain by confirming his belief that the meaning question is indeed essential to life. A philosopher like Schopenhauer would confirm his conviction that life was nothing but ultimate misery. "It is all—vanity! Happy is he who has not been born: death is better than life, and one must free oneself".

Fine-tuning faith and avoiding the ultimate failure

For Tolstoy, rationally speaking, the only reasonable answer to his existential question could come from faith. However, he had denounced Christianity at an early age because he found it to be irrational. It was a paradoxical situation. He had difficulty in accepting the irrational elements of the Christian faith: "God, One in Three; the creation in six days; the devils and angels, and all the rest that I cannot accept as long as I retain my reason" (*A Confession*, Chapter 8). However, he had no choice but to be selective, by rejecting the irrational creed of Christianity, while accepting the rational part. He came to believe in God but rejected the notion of the Trinity. He embraced sincere prayer but condemned eating bread with wine as a symbol of Jesus's flesh and blood. He even came up with his own Bible by combining major books of Christianity while filtering irrational elements.

$$H_{e1} = \{U\ (H, D, B, L) + M\ (H, D, B, L)\}\ *F = 0 \text{ if } F = 0$$

Tolstoy's life story was a perfect confession confirming our happiness equation. In his early life, Tolstoy pursued hedonic pleasure by trying to maximize his utility through having, doing, and being. It did not take long for him to realize that it was not possible to reach life satisfaction through hedonic happiness. He extended his happiness equation by adding the meaning term through authorship and family. He became a worldwide famous novelist. Millions were reading his novels. He was also a dedicated parent, raising 13 children with a loving wife. Though he was better off for a while in terms of his life satisfaction, he could not stop asking existential questions which made everything seem ultimately meaningless. He was in his fifties when he noticed that the F multiplier would make everything zero if F was equal to zero. Thus, for him, the only way out from the meaning crisis was to add faith to his equation. He needed a faith that could kill death as the ultimate destroyer; link finite to infinite, and connect human to the Creator.

We agree with Tolstoy that it is not possible to reach authentic happiness without faith, which brings transcendental meaning. As expressed in the happiness equation, temporal meaning extends life satisfaction, but not enough to bring ultimate satisfaction. Of course, one can live in denial of the ultimate meaning. However, this will not change the inevitable reality. It will be only self-deception. As Tolstoy honestly confessed, it seems impossible to live in such denial for an entire life. Sooner or later, we will be reminded that everything is ultimately meaningless if there is no faith in life after death. Indeed, Taylor argued that we cannot avoid falling into a great crisis whenever we face the reality of death. "The deepest, most powerful kind of happiness, even in the moment, is plunged into a sense of meaning. And the meaning seems denied by certain kinds of ending. That's why the greatest crisis around death comes from the death of someone we love" (Taylor 2007, Chapter 19).

We argue that, for atheists, everything is ultimately meaningless. They cannot find lasting happiness if they live a life without faith. For instance, Stephen Hawking lived a very successful life. One might think of his life as fulfilled, given his success despite adversities. According to the happiness model above, it is not possible to count Hawking as a happy person because he did not have any faith. He was not fortunate in terms of pursuing happiness through doing. However, he did succeed greatly in being a very famous scientist. He was a best-selling author. He made a significant contribution to science. Thus, his meaning from being was very high. None of those are sufficient to claim that he had a fulfilled life with great satisfaction. As an atheist, he claimed that the F multiplier was zero. Thus, he knew that the F would make everything be zero eventually. He lived in denial of this fact and did not commit suicide. However, in the end, everything became absolute zero for him from his perspective. He did not believe in the soul. As a pure materialist, he was doomed to be decomposed back to its elements as if he never existed. It was just a wave-like reality that temporarily took the form of a being called Stephen Hawking; then, it disappeared forever. The very moment he experienced death, all of his accomplishments died with him, in terms of being meaningless for him. In the end, if there is no life after death and no punishment for his disbelief, the best outcome he accomplished in life was zero.

Conclusion

It is a common human experience to begin examining the meaning of life as we get older. As we get older, we become more convinced that having, doing, and being cannot bring life satisfaction. In my personal journey, I was not satisfied with temporal meaning, either. I began contemplating more on the transcendental meaning of my life. I personally did not experience a midlife crisis because my happiness equation has included faith since the very early age of my life. As I advanced in my education, I did not give up my faith. Instead, I learned how to compromise science and faith. My worldview allows me to consider true science as the deciphering of God's acts in the universe. I learned how to read the universe as an elegant book written by the pen of Divine Power. To me, scientific knowledge is a way to know more about God's acts and attributes. I have developed a strong affirmation about the existence of God, who is All-Knowing, All-Powerful, All-Wise, Most-Kind, Most-Loving. Therefore, it does not make sense that He would let our life be annihilated with death. I believe He will maintain our life in some form after death. This faith brings transcendental meaning to my life. It gives me the power to continue my work without fear of being annihilated at any moment. In the next chapter, I will discuss how believing brought the ultimate satisfaction in my life.

PART IV
SEEKING HAPPINESS IN SPIRITUAL (G-DONIC) DIMENSION

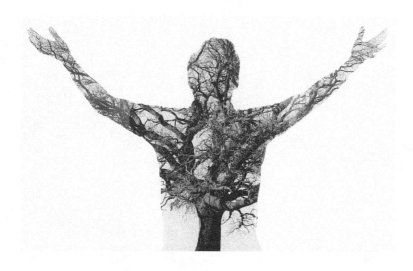

Chapter 14

Searching for G-donic Happiness through Believing

"God will not deceive me nor allow me to be deceived as long as I do my best to get at the truth"

—Descartes

Defining G-donic Dimension of Happiness

The G-donic dimension is centered around the firm belief in the existence of God and the hereafter. We argue that knowing, meaning, and believing are the necessary elements of a happy life within the G-donic model. Knowing means realizing. It means knowing the ultimate reality behind observed phenomena. It means finding answers to extensional questions such as: Who am I? What is the ultimate reality? Why am I here? Meaning refers to transcendental purpose. It requires living a purpose-driven life. It means knowing what is worth living for. It involves pursuing meaning maximization in the daily life experience of having, doing, and being. Believing means having an evidence-based conviction that God is the source of experienced reality.

We define happiness in the G-donic model as inner tranquility achieved through remembrance of God. That is only possible if one perceives the convincing evidence of God in the universe through His ongoing creative actions. We think G-donic happiness applies to all religions that believe in an All-Knowing and All-Powerful God who creates and sustains the phenomenal reality and promises to give eternal life after death. We argue that living conscious of God by remembering Him through his actions is the key to authentic happiness.

By the remembrance of God, we do NOT mean the utterance of God by word only; rather, we mean transcendental consciousness in which one becomes aware of the ultimate reality behind the phenomenal one. Thus, we define G-donic happiness based on the perception of the reality of the self, others, and the universe through belief in God and the hereafter. It means believing in God as the true and ultimate reality behind phenomenal reality. While God is necessarily existent, everything else is contingent upon His existence, like shadow and origin. Thus, from G-donic perspective, the human is born into shadow like phenomenal reality. Becoming a believer means to bear witness to this reality and live life accordingly. The goal is to read the book of the universe and feel the presence of God in everything. Since it is not possible to gain satisfaction through shadow, human nature will only find peace and contentment once he/she finds God through perceiving transcendental reality. Therefore, belief is not defined as the acceptance of God as an unknown Supreme Being. Instead, it is defined as the belief in God as the Creator and Sustainer of everything. Once one becomes convinced that God is the ultimate reality and everything else just His manifestation, lasting happiness is possible for him/her but depends on the degree of the realization of such transcendental reality. As such a person achieves certainty in such realization, he/she will accomplish authentic happiness from God.

G-donic happiness is based on a theological ontology that puts God at the center of reality. From this perspective, G-donic happiness is much higher than other types of happiness because it takes people to a higher dimension of perceived reality. It is a way to get beyond phenomenal reality and see transcendental reality, in which everything is controlled, created, and sustained by God. It is a way of perceiving God as Necessary Existent behind shadowy-like contingent existence. Even Paradise is nothing but a manifestation of God's names. We think *Flatland* (Abbott 1963), a book written two centuries ago, serves a great example to understand how G-donic happiness might take people to a higher dimension. The book is an attempt to explain the difference between two and three-dimensional worlds. Some characters in the book are born in the two-dimensional world.

For them, there is only height and length. There is no depth. There is just left and right at the same level. Everything is flat. There is no up and down. When one character in the two-dimensional world encountered the one in a three-dimensional world, he was puzzled to learn that you could look from above and see what is going to happen. Likewise, in the G-donic model, a believer is supposed to wear multi-dimensional glasses to perceive transcendental reality. As one reflects on the internal (subjective) and external (objective) signs (ayah) of God, one would feel His presence and feel peace and happiness, since whatever He does is either directly or indirectly good. In such a case, everything gains infinite significance. As Kierkegaard said, "To me, it seems … that to be known in time by God makes life enormously strenuous. Everywhere where he is present, each half hour is of infinite importance. "(Concluding Unscientific Postscript)

The G-donic model assumes that we perceive transcendental meaning and beauty in everything. As a result, everything becomes extremely valuable art and bounty. For instance, for a person with no knowledge of art, it is hard to appreciate the true value of the Mona Lisa portrait. He might even throw it into the trash. However, once he becomes aware of its art and market value, he would treasure this piece of art. Similarly, through the transcendental belief, if we perceive God's signature on his inimitable artifacts, we will appreciate them with great admiration. Indeed, we will realize the true value of everything with respect to its Maker.

The perception of transcendental meaning brings tremendous value to everything. In this regard, we are like the fisherman from the Philippines who found a pearl but did not use for a long time because of not knowing its true value[14]. He kept it under his bed for almost 10 years. Finally, after an accidental

---

14   https://www.forbes.com/sites/trevornace/2016/09/28/fisherman-100-million-pearl-good-luck-charm/#34ad51801670, accessed on December 27, 2018.

fire destroyed his home, he took the pearl to the market and learned that it was worth $100 million. We argue belief brings true enrichment to believers by revealing the true value of everything in life. In reality, we all live in our own world, which is built upon our perception. Thus, if we perceive everything as precious artifacts of Infinite Power, Infinite Wisdom, and Infinite Beauty, we will derive tremendous pleasure from this transcendental meaning.

Faith and Happiness for Transcendental Believers

Using Plato's cave metaphor discussed before, we can define transcendental believers as those who transcend the shadow and find the reality. But how? We think that it is possible by studying the nature of shadow. In that story, the prisoners were not able to see the source of shadows. They could hear the sounds, but they were thinking that the sounds were coming from the observed shadows. If they had studied the shadows carefully, they might have realized that the difference between shadows could not produce different sounds since, in reality, the nature of shadow is the same, but the shape differs. They might have realized that the nature of shadow is not able to produce any sound if they compare properties of the shadow with their own qualities.

Similarly, in this world, as is well-documented in science when we study the profound reality of matter, we will find out that everything is made primarily of same essential fundamental components such as electrons and protons. The only difference between fundamental elements in the universe is the number of electrons and protons. For instance, what makes hydrogen different from oxygen is that the former has one electron while the latter has eight. If we go further down in the subatomic world, we will find that the same basic ingredients such as quarks or strings are the source of material reality. Thus, similar to the shadow in the cave story, all observed differences are composed out of one thing. As it is not possible to ascribe different sounds only to varying sizes of shadows, it is not reasonable to assume different objects are anything but the outcome of different number of basic elements.

Furthermore, the properties of the effect have nothing to do with the properties of causes. For instance, salt is made of sodium and chlorine. Both elements are poisonous if they are consumed alone. However, strangely, when they come together, they become a necessary substance for the human body. In reality, if we combine two different poisons, we will get an even stronger poison, not necessary nutrition. Thus, as we study the nature of cause and effect, we shall realize that the observed causal relationship is like a shadow that cannot be responsible for the effect. The effect comes from transcendental reality, not observed phenomena.

The distinguishing trait of transcendental believers is that they have a conviction about the transcendental reality. The conviction could be based on verified evidence or self-conviction without any evidence. As long as they are convinced that there is an ultimate reality behind the shadows, they will not seek satisfaction through the shadow-like world by having, doing, being, and meaning. They will seek satisfaction through transcendental reality behind them. Of course, it is not easy to identify the type of faith people have. We think the attitude toward death is a good measure of one's faith. Skeptical believers would have higher death anxiety compared to transcendental believers.

Furthermore, transcendental believers would look forward to dying while skeptical believers would love to live forever in this world. Transcendental believers also reflect on the endless blessing of the All-Loving Maker of the universe. They feel endless appreciation as they think that they are special guests benefiting from aspects of the entire universe.

Belief as a multiplier

For transcendental believers, faith is not an additive term. It is the ultimate determinant of utility and meaning from having, doing, and being. It adds a new dimension to eudemonic happiness. It reveals the transcendental reality behind the shadowy reality in this life. Thus, it encourages its followers to pursue satisfaction through transcendental reality, not its transient reflection. It puts God at the source of reality and the center of happiness-seeking. Therefore, we call this model the G-donic happiness model, which differs significantly from both hedonic and eudemonic happiness models. We define the happiness equation for the transcendental believers within the G-donic model as follows:

$$H_g = \{U\ (H,\ B,\ D) + M\ (H,\ D,\ B)\} *F_t$$

Transcendental believers do not seek worldly satisfaction through having, doing, being, meaning, and the believing as an added term. Using the caveman metaphor, they believe that there is a reality behind the shadows and pursue the reality rather than the shadows. Once they perceive the transcendental reality, they change their attitude toward the shadowy reality of having, doing, being, and meaning. For them, faith can transform everything, including a painful experience, into a pleasant one.

On the other hand, without transcendental meaning ($F_t = 0$), everything loses its ultimate meaning. As shown in the graph below, believing brings new dimension to transcendental believers. It transforms having, doing, being, and meaning based on perceived transcendental reality.

Figure 1. G-donic Happiness Dimensions with Having, Doing, Being, Loving, Meaning, & Believing (t)

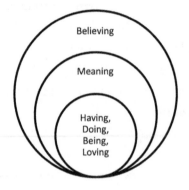

Transcendental believers can achieve life satisfaction in this world because they believe that life is not going to end with death. Their worldly satisfaction depends on their level of certainty in such a belief through realizing transcendental reality behind the shadowy reality. As they reflect and remember this reality, they are sure that their lives will continue after death. Thus, they will be satisfied by believing they have eternal life. As their utility and meaning from having, doing, being, is going to approach infinity over time, they will have full satisfaction in life. In other words, their happiness function of $H_g = \{U (H, D, B, L) + M (H, D,$

B, L)} *F_t is going to approach infinity over time if they have a conviction about eternal life after death:

$$H_g = \infty \text{ if } F_t = \infty$$

Tolstoy's Search for Happiness through Transcendental Faith

Though Tolstoy knew faith as an addition to the happiness equation, he was not satisfied with that. He knew that the ultimate end would be the same if he followed the Church as a skeptic believer without having any conviction about God. Indeed, without God, he felt a "feeling of fear, orphanage, isolation in a strange land." When he was at the edge of ending his agony, he had "a hope of help from someone." He described his painful midlife crisis as nothing but the search for God with conviction: "During that whole year, when I was asking myself almost every moment whether I should not end matters with a noose or a bullet—all that time, together with the course of thought and observation about which I have spoken, my heart was oppressed with a painful feeling, which I can only describe as a search for God."

Tolstoy failed to gain conviction through the religious teaching available to him. He pursued natural theology by perceiving the evidence of God's existence from the universe. "Cause, said I to myself, is not a category of thought such as are Time and Space. If I exist, there must be some cause for it, and a cause of causes. And that first cause of all is what men have called 'God.' And I paused on that thought and tried with all my being to recognize the presence of that cause. And as soon as I acknowledged that there is a force in whose power I am, I at once felt that I could live. But I asked myself: What is that cause, that force? How am I to think of it? What are my relations to that which I call 'God'? And only the familiar replies occurred to me: 'He is the Creator and Preserver.'"

Tolstoy felt great joy as soon as he concluded that God does exist. "I had only for an instant to admit that, and at once life rose within me, and I felt the possibility and joy of being." However, this feeling did not last long. He wanted to know God and established a relationship with Him. "From the admission of the existence of a God I went on to seek my relationship with

Him." He could not grasp the idea of the Trinity. He could not rationally accept that God could be Three Persons, "Again I imagined *that* God—our Creator in Three Persons who sent His Son, the Savior—and again *that* God." As Tolstoy would think about Trinitarian god, he would again fall into despair that perhaps there was no god. "Not three times, but tens and hundreds of times, I reached those conditions, first of joy and animation, and then of despair and consciousness of the impossibility of living." His hope and despair of finding God lasted three years: "I listened and thought ever of the same thing, as I had constantly done during those last three years. I was again seeking God. 'Very well, there is no God,' said I to myself; 'there is no one who is not my imagination but a reality like my whole life. He does not exist, and no miracles can prove His existence, because the miracles would be my imagination, besides being irrational.'"

Indeed, he stated that the irrational teaching of the Church was pushing him away from the idea of God. Whenever he attended a service at a church, he had to ignore the following Trinitarian belief because it did not make sense to him: "In unity, we believe in the Father, the Son, and the Holy Ghost." He tried to make sense of this statement, but without any success: "When I forced an explanation into them, [it] made me feel that I was lying, thereby quite destroying my relation to God and depriving me of all possibility of belief."

Tolstoy began appealing to God directly. Asking Him for help. He believed that if God existed, he would help him in his search. He felt like a baby who had lost his mother and was "lying on my back crying in the high grass, even then I cry because I know that a mother has borne me within her, has hatched me, warmed me, fed me." He began praying for help. However, he said, "the more I prayed, the more apparent it became to me that He did not hear me and that there was no one to whom to address myself. And with despair in my heart that there is no God at all, I said: 'Lord, have mercy, save me! Lord, teach me!' But no one had mercy on me, and I felt that my life was coming to a standstill." He could not see any reason to maintain his life if there was no God. "I do not live when I lose belief in the existence of God. I should long ago have killed myself had I not had a dim hope of finding Him. I live, really live, only when I feel Him and seek Him." He eventually found conviction through his inner voice: "'What more do you seek?' exclaimed a voice within me. "'This is He. He is that without which one cannot live'".

For Tolstoy, once a person found God, he had to give up worldly life. "He must live 'godly'" and to live 'godly' he must renounce all the pleasures of life, must labor, humble himself, suffer, and be merciful." Thus, everything gains meaning because they could no longer be destroyed by death as long as they are godly. Indeed, for Tolstoy, "The essence of every faith consists in its giving life a meaning which death does not destroy."

Human Nature and G-donic Happiness

Primarily inspired by the writings of some Muslim scholars such as Al-Ghazali and Nursi, we developed a new theory of human nature: 'A Grand Theory of Human Nature (GTHN)', using the RV and resident metaphors that follow (Aydin, 2012a). The theory helps us to understand the G-donic happiness model. The theory compares the human body to a luxury recreational vehicle (RV) to explain the following elements of human nature as the residents in that vehicle: *King, Judge, Wazir, Elephant, Showman, Dog, and, Driver.* The *King* is the spiritual heart that is the source of love and inspirational knowledge. The *Judge* is the conscience that is the source of positive feelings after performing 'good things' and negative feelings experienced after doing 'bad things. The *Wazir (prime minister)* is the mind. The *Elephant* is the animal spirit, which is the source of animalistic desires. The *Showman* is the self-centric ego that pursues power and possession to show its importance to others. The *Dog* is an inner drive for protection of personal belongings with the potential to oppress others for their possessions. The *Driver* is the deciding self (free will) that drives the vehicle under the influence of the residents.

From a comprehensive point of view, one could not use the pronoun 'I' anymore while defining one's happiness. There is not one entity as self. One should talk about selves referring to multiple residents presented above. In this regard, we are not just the '*reasoning self* (mind/the Wazir)', we are also the '*spiritual self* (the heart/the King)', '*moral self* (the conscience/ the Judge)', '*animal self* (the animal soul/the Elephant)', '*showing-off self* (the self-centric ego/ the Showman)', '*oppressive self* (the oppressive ego/ the Dog)', and '*deciding *self* (the free will/ the Driver)'. Therefore, one needs to know one SELVES holistically to make one SELVES happy. We could briefly discuss the needs and desires of the seven residents as follows. The King has almost an infinite capacity to love. He needs/desires beauty, perfection, and benefits in his lover(s). From his perspective, life is a journey of making attachments to satisfy these needs. Attachments can be made to material and/or immaterial things such as money, property, lovers, friends, nature, and God. The judge wants fairness and justice in life and would cause moral pleasure if we treat others and are treated fairly. He would make us feel moral pain if we engage in unfair acts. The *Wazir* (mind) pursues knowledge and receives intellectual pleasure from learning. He performs the role of making rational decisions for the *King* and other residents such as the *Elephant* and the *Judge*. However, he has no power to endorse his decision and may be silenced if the *Elephant* is too strong. The *Elephant* is the greedy, animal nature of the human being. The *Elephant* has the capacity for sensual experience through using the five senses. He needs and/or desires many things such as food, drink, sleep, sex, etc. The *Showman* is motivated by acts that produce recognition and fame. He frequently compares his own possessions with those of others. The *Dog* is the power to control and rule others. If he is not constrained by moral and legal codes, he will oppress others for his interests. The *Driver* is the deciding self or free will, which is the ultimate decision maker in the RV. He is the one in control of the vehicle. However, his actions are influenced by other residents.

The G-donic model perceives happiness as the way we deal with the residents above rather than as a destination. In other words, happiness is the experience while driving on the happiness highway. Happiness is the byproduct of living according to God's pleasure. Using the RV analogy, we can define happiness as overall life satisfaction for the residents of the RV while driving on the straight path. In other words, happiness is to drive the RV under the collaborative command of the *King* (heart), *Judge* (conscience), and *Wazir* (mind). It is to drive toward excellence with sincere spiritual, intellectual, and moral intentions and actions. It is to keep the *Elephant* (animal soul), *Dog* (anger), and *Showman* (egoistic self) under the command of the King, Wazir, and Judge. It is to establish our inner kingdom upon intellectual, moral, and spiritual wealth.

While the G-donic model guides and nourishes the heart, mind, and intellect, it also highlights the danger of being a slave to the animal soul, ego, and anger. It warns people that if not trained, the *Elephant, Showman,* and *Dog* will dominate the RV and urge certain irrational actions despite any objection from the *King, Wazir,* and *Judge.* The G-donic model provides nourishment for the *King* who has the capacity for love, compassion, and inspiration. It guides people on how to find authentic and lasting love in life for the fulfillment of the *King.* It discusses the role of loving mates, children, friends and jobs in the pursuit of happiness.

The G-donic model notes that the inner *Judge* (conscience) always makes a judgment about what we do to others. If we treat someone unfairly, he causes us to be aware of this injustice and feel guilty for being unfair. If we treat others fairly, we receive spiritual pleasure experienced through the fulfillment of the judge. The G-donic model presents the food station for the *Wazir* who is thirsty for knowledge and meaning. Finding meaning in life is very important for the Wazir because as the navigator, he needs to know where to go. Life without meaning is like driving without knowing the destination. The G-donic model also offers a guide on how to keep the animal soul, showman, and dog under control. It suggests moderation in consumption and warns about the poisons present in some food. It makes some recommendations for pleasure maximization under restraints of the 'law of diminishing marginal utility,' 'adaptation principle,' and the 'hedonic treadmill.'

The happiness function based on the G-donic model captures six different dimensions of the human experience as represented by the residents of the vehicle. For instance, happiness for the King depends on how one fulfills the needs/desires of love, compassion, and inspiration. Love pursues beauty, perfection, and benefits. Life for the *King* in this regard is a journey of making attachments. The number, intensity, and duration of attachments produce spiritual or esthetic pleasures. As the *King* gains pleasure by making attachments through love, compassion, and inspiration, he also suffers from any detachments that occur. Like the *King,* each resident of the human vehicle experiences pain and/or pleasure from daily activities. Therefore, we could define happiness as a function of subjective well-being for all residents in the matrix as shown below:

$$H= \sum w_i h_i(X_i) = w_1 h_1(K) + w_2 h_2(J) +$$
$$w_3 h_3(W) + w_4 h_4(E) + w_5 h_5(D) - w_6 h_6(S)$$

Where H is one's overall satisfaction with life, w_i is the weight of a specific happiness variable if one is overall happy with life, h_1 is one's happiness function with the *King*, h_2 is one's happiness function with the *Judge*, h_3 is one's happiness function with the *Wazir*, h_4 is one's happiness function with the *Elephant*, h_5 is one's happiness function with the *Dog*, and h_6 is one's happiness function with the *Showman*. Therefore, overall life satisfaction is maximized when the needs and desires of the first five are fulfilled in a balanced way while the effect of the last one (*the Showman*) is minimized.

Conclusion

The three-dimensional happiness model suggests that we need to move to a higher dimension for higher life satisfaction. We argue that being in a higher dimension brings higher life satisfaction regardless of how much we achieve in terms of having, doing, being, and loving. Thus, our primary objective should be on the dimensions rather than on possession, participation, and position. If we live in the hedonic dimension, it is not possible to gain satisfaction through having, doing, being, and loving, even if we succeed in getting what we like most in life. We will eventually hit the dead end after trying many different things, due to the DEAD loop of deprivation, emulation, achievement, and disappointment. This phenomenon is well captured in the research and known as the "hedonic treadmill". We cannot reach the destination of authentic happiness with the hedonic happiness function. In reality, many people hit the dead end while trying to be happy with some having, doing, being, and loving. However, they think if they try again with different things, they might have a different outcome. Thus, they would repeat the DEAD hedonic loop with many things in life. Most people come to understand the loop by the time they reach their mid-life. Some quit playing the game, but some keep repeating until their death. We can move to a higher dimension by adding meaning to our happiness function. This will bring us higher satisfaction.

In the second dimension, we do not aim to maximize pleasure only to reach life satisfaction. Rather, we also will try to maximize the meaning of having, doing, being, and loving. Pleasure is not our primary objective. We will be fine with something meaningful, but painful. We argue that staying in this dimension will not bring the ultimate life satisfaction, either. Eventually, we will hit the dead end because it is no different from the hedonic loop regarding its phases of deprivation, emulation, achievement, and disappointment. Perhaps, the loop is longer. Therefore, it takes more time to realize that it is a treadmill. Meaning brings enrichment to our life by adding a new dimension to our experience of having, doing, and being. As shown in Figure 2 below, the marginal utility from the meaning dimension is increasing up to a certain point. As we give more importance to meaning, we will explore the ultimate meaning of our efforts. If we have no belief in the afterlife, we will soon realize that we face an ultimately meaningless life. That is when our marginal utility of meaning will begin heading down to be flat at zero. We will not be satisfied with temporal meaning, but ultimate meaninglessness. We argue that once the marginal utility of meaning hits the bottom, we will fall into depression and desperation. That is the dead end. We must seek another dimension to sustain our life journey.

We argue that we can move to the third dimension through faith. We do not mean blind faith or wishful thinking. We define faith as connecting finite to infinite. It is to find the transcendental reality behind the observed phenomena in this world. It is to reach a conviction that life will continue after death. We argue that once we reach such realization, we will change our attitude toward the worldly having, doing, being, and loving. We will no longer seek satisfaction with a shadow-like earthly reality. Instead, we will find satisfaction with transcendental reality.

As seen in Figure 2, we argue that the long-term marginal utility of transcendental spirituality (TS) is upsloping. Unlike the marginal utility from the eudemonic dimension, the one for the TS dimension does not have to fall as long as we sustain our conviction in life after death. Since at the TS level, we experience the third dimension in addition to pleasure and meaning dimensions, we can reach very high satisfaction at almost any condition. In other words, if we add the depth of spiritual experience to our worldly experience of having, doing, being, and meaning, we could potentially derive infinite satisfaction at every level. In modern times, we tend to live on the surface rather than delve into the deep meaning of existence. Mathematically speaking, if we add the third dimension (depth) to the green line below, we can potentially reach a very high level of satisfaction with any level of resources. We do not have to be rich, healthy, young, or famous. We will find infinite richness in life experience at almost any condition as long as we delve into the third dimension.

Figure 2. Long-term Marginal Utility of Transcendental Spirituality

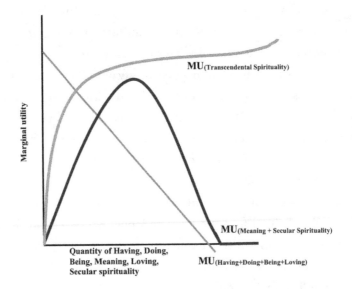

It is important to note that once we discover the third dimension, it does not mean that we will live in that dimension all the time. Indeed, as a human, we will still experience the first and second dimensions. The law of diminishing marginal utility for the first dimension is still applicable to us when we pursue bodily pleasures. However, we can always jump to the third dimension and derive higher satisfaction. We need to have reflective spiritual meditation to delve into the third dimension. Thus, we need to learn how to transcend from shadow-like phenomenal reality to transcendental reality through knowledge and reflection.

Chapter 15

Scientific Research of G-donic Happiness

"Belief necessitates affirmation of Divine unity, an affirmation of Divine unity necessitates submission to God, submission to God necessitates reliance on God, and reliance on God necessarily leads to happiness in this world and the next"

—Nursi

Introduction

Though many studies point to the importance of spirituality for a meaningful and fulfilled life, no systematic research has been conducted on G-donic happiness. That is because we are the first ones who conceptualized the G-donic dimension. We have done empirical studies to test our hypotheses. In this chapter, we will share the findings from two relevant studies.

First, we will present the findings from a study we conducted in the Gulf countries to measure the contribution of each dimension to the overall subjective wellbeing and daily happiness. Then, we will share the findings of an empirical study we conducted among the followers of Said Nursi, a prominent 20th-century scholar from Turkey, whom we consider to be a leading figure of G-donic happiness.

First Study: Comparison of Three Dimensions

In Spring 2019, with a group of students, we conducted a comprehensive survey to explore comparative evidence for three dimensions of happiness. We used the questionnaire provided in the bonus page. The survey consisted of four parts: demographic questions, happiness dimension questions, luxury consumption, and subjective wellbeing questions. In total, 230 people with diverse demographic profiles responded to the survey. It is important to note that the majority of participants were between 18 and 40 years old.

For the hedonic dimension, we asked six questions. We used a 6-level Likert scale to assess the responses, 1 stands for the lowest while 6 for the highest. After confirming the relevance of the questions through the factor analysis, we calculated the hedonic dimension (HD) score for each individual based on the cumulative score of the six questions.

For the eudemonic dimension, we had six questions. The factor loading statistics confirmed the relevance of those questions to the eudemonic dimension. Therefore, the individual eudemonic dimension (ED) score was calculated based on the cumulative score from those questions. Likewise, we calculated the G-donic dimension score for each individual based on their corresponding score for the six G-donic related questions. Finally, the cumulative luxury consumption score was calculated based on three relevant questions. The descriptive statistics for those variables are shown in the table below.

Descriptive Statistics				
	HD Score	ED Score	LC Score	GD Score
Mean	25.2	29.6	13.5	30.3
Median	25	30	13	32
Std. Deviation	4.9	3.8	3.2	4.6
Minimum	13	14	6	10
Maximum	35	36	20	36

For wellbeing, we used three different indicators: First, cumulative subjective wellbeing based on the score from six relevant questions; Second, a more direct question of assessing one's overall happiness using a ten-point scale of happiness ladder (zero = absolutely miserable life while ten = a perfectly happy life); Third, a ten-point scale of assessing present-day happiness.

Increasing Subjective Wellbeing through an Increase within Each Dimension

For comparison, we divided each dimension into two categories: high and low. Those who scored below the mean for each dimension were considered to be low while those who scored above the average were considered high in that dimension. Based on the survey data, as seen in the chart below, if you move from the low hedonic to high hedonic level, on average, you will increase your subjective wellbeing by five percent. On the other hand, if you move to high eudemonic, your subjective wellbeing will go up by 17 percent. You can experience an even higher increase if you shift from the low to a high level within the G-donic dimension. In other words, if you try to be more hedonic, you might increase your happiness a little bit. However, if you expand your eudemonic or G-donic dimension, you will experience a substantial increase in your subjective wellbeing. Obviously, if you invest in both eudemonic and G-donic dimensions, you will have a real boost in your happiness.

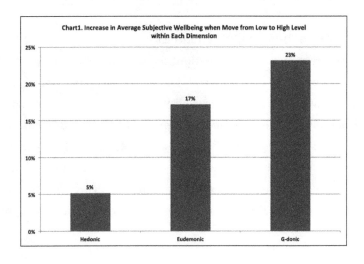

Achieving the Highest Happiness in the Present Day

Using the response to the question about rating the present-day happiness based on a 0-10 scale, we calculated the likelihood of having the highest happiness (scoring 9 or 10). As seen in the chart below, moving from low to high hedonic level would make virtually no difference in terms of achieving the highest level of happiness at the present day. On the other hand, if you move from the low to a high level within the eudemonic dimension, you are 2.4 times more likely to achieve the highest happiness at the present day. The likelihood is even higher, 2.6 times, for a similar shift within the G-donic dimension.

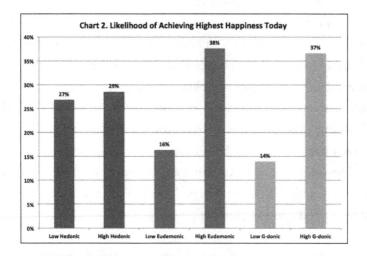

Achieving the Highest Happiness in Life

Based on the response to the question about rating overall life satisfaction using a ten-point scale of happiness ladder, we calculated the likelihood of achieving the highest happiness (scoring 9 or 10). As seen in the chart below, moving from low to high hedonic level would make a clear difference in terms of achieving the highest level of happiness. Your chance of being at the top of the ladder is 15 percent, regardless of whether you are hedonic or not. On the other hand, if you move from the low to a high level within the eudemonic dimension, you are 3.1 times more likely to achieve the highest happiness in terms of overall satisfaction in life. The likelihood is even higher, 3.3 times, for a similar shift within the G-donic dimension. Comparing with the previous chart, it is obvious that being high in the hedonic dimension helps in present-day happiness, but not for the overall life satisfaction when we reflect on the entire life. On the other hand, any enhancement in the eudemonic or G-donic dimension help to have higher happiness at the present day and life in total. The positive contribution is way higher in the long-run compared to the present-day experience.

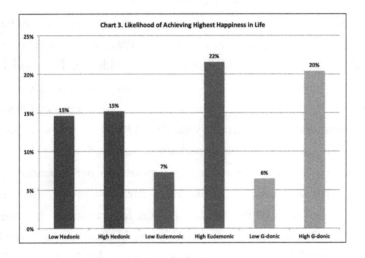

As stated before, participants were relatively young compared to the general population. As seen in the table below, the correlation between age and hedonic dimension was negative, meaning that as people get older they are less likely to be hedonic. Likewise, the correlation between age and luxury consumption (LC) was also negative. On the other hand, the correlation between age and G-donic dimension was positive meaning that as people get older they are more likely to pursue the spiritual dimension. Thus, it is fair to argue that the study overestimates the impact of hedonic dimension while underestimates the impact of G-donic dimension due to age bias of the sample.

Table 2. Pearson Correlation Between Age,
Happiness Dimensions, and Consumption

		Hedonic Dimension	Eudemonic Dimension	G-donic Dimension	Cum. LC Score
Age	Pearson Correlation	-.259**	-.009	.261**	-.174**
	Sig. (2-tailed)	.000	.889	.000	.008
	N	235	231	229	235

Regression Results for Three Dimensions

We run three different regressions using the three different measures of happiness above. The first linear regression model explored the relationship between several independent variables and cumulative subjective wellbeing. The coefficients for both luxury consumption and hedonic dimension variables were statistically insignificant. This means we could not claim any statistically significant impact of those variables on the subjective wellbeing. On the other hand, coefficients for both eudemonic and G-donic dimensions were statistically highly significant. They both seem to have almost the same impact on the dependent variable. All other variables turned out to be statistically insignificant. The result was very similar when we used the happiness ladder for present-day happiness. The hedonic dimension was statistically insignificant in those models as well, while eudemonic and G-donic dimensions were found to be significant and highly effective in determining happiness level.

Second Study: Spirituality and Subjective Wellbeing among Nursi Readers

While materialism attempts to fulfill the sensual desires of human beings through conspicuous consumption, Said Nursi, who was an influential spiritual leader, suggested a happiness model through moderate material consumption and spiritual nourishment.

Nursi challenged consumer culture with his writings and simple lifestyle. He argued that "absolute vice" was being called civilization and he was severely critical of this "dissolute civilization" which promotes a consumer culture. In his view, modern civilization casts humanity down to the level of animals: "… its alluring service is to excite lust and the appetites of the soul and facilitate the gratification of whims, and their result is vice." The mark of lust and passion is always this: "They transform a man into a beast, changing his character; they deform him, perverting his humanity"(Nursi 1996, 745).

Nursi argues that believing, knowing, loving God is the way to lasting happiness. He believes that life without God would be meaningless, fruitless, painful: "The person who knows and loves God Almighty may receive endless bounties, happiness, lights, and mysteries. While the one who does not truly know and love him is afflicted spiritually and materially by endless *misery, pain, and fears*. Even if such an impotent, miserable person owned the whole world, it would be *worth nothing* for him, for it would seem to him that he was living a *fruitless life* among the vagrant human race in a wretched world without owner or protector [emphasis added]" (Nursi, 1996a, 20th Letter).

In his answer to a question asked by many on the secret for the success of his books, Nursi points out that in good deeds and virtues and spirituality are to be found pleasures, like the pleasures of Paradise. In 2010, with Eron Manusov from Duke University, we conducted a comprehensive survey among Nursi followers to test Nursi's happiness claim within the G-donic model(Aydin and Manusov 2014). We designed the survey in a way to capture the values and goals of individuals within 14 different domains. This measurement allowed for the assessment of the relative centrality of particular goals/values within an individual's personal goal/value system.

The Research Design

The questionnaire was sent to 1523 followers of Nursi identified by the Istanbul Science and Culture Foundation, a foundation with a mission of promoting Said Nursi's views. The response rate was 32% (489 people).

The survey consisted of three sections. The first section included 13 questions about demographic information, such as gender, age, level of education, household income, and marital status, the frequency of reading Nursi's books and participating in the relevant activities. The second section included 86 questions aimed to capture the frequency of certain activities within 14 life domains using a 9-point Likert-type scale. This section reproduced the well-known Aspiration Index that captures eleven domains of human experience: self-acceptance, affiliation, community feeling, security, health, spirituality, financial success, image, popularity, hedonism, and conformity. (Kasser, T. (2007).

Our survey added three more domains, namely intellectual life, honesty and fairness, and aesthetic experience. The third section of the survey captures three sets of questions on life satisfaction, needs, and pleasures. For comparison, the participants were divided into three subgroups based on their reading of Nursi's books and engagement in the spiritual activities: the beginner, the intermediate, and the advanced Nursi readers.

The Aspiration Index (AI) of Nursi Readers

The AI results revealed that spirituality, fairness and honesty, affiliation, intellectual activities, self-acceptance, and personal growth, aesthetics experience, conformity, community feeling, and physical health have positive mean-corrected scores. The mean score for all goal/value domains mentioned was consistently higher for higher levels of Nursi readers. In other words, the more they read Nursi and are involved in relevant activities, the greater the importance they place on the values relevant to eudemonic and G-donic dimensions. On the other hand, hedonism, popularity, and fame, money, image, security, and fear had negative mean-corrected scores for all three levels of Nursi readers. Again, the negative scores were consistently greater for higher levels of Nursi readers. The more they read Nursi, the less importance they place on the hedonic dimension. In other words, the survey result revealed that Nursi readers give great importance to eudemonic and G-donic dimensions in seeking happiness.

Chart 4 captures the world value/goal system for the advanced level of Nursi readers. Based on the mean-corrected importance scores, the figure shows that the advanced level Nursi readers place greater importance on spirituality, honesty and fairness, family and friendship, intellectual activities, personal growth while they try to stay away from hedonic, egoistic, and materialistic goals/values.

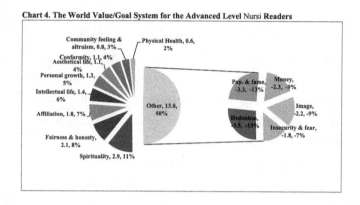

Chart 4. The World Value/Goal System for the Advanced Level Nursi Readers

Subjective Well-being of the Nursi Readers

We used the Satisfaction with Life Scale (SWLS) to measure the subjective well-being of Nursi readers. The SWLS is a short 5-item instrument designed to measure global cognitive judgments of satisfaction with one's life.

According to a comprehensive life satisfaction survey conducted by the Turkish Statistical Institute in 2010, 54% of people were satisfied with their lives. In response to the comparable question in our study, 62% of the beginner, 82% of the intermediate, and 93% of the advanced group members were satisfied with their lives as seen in the chart below.

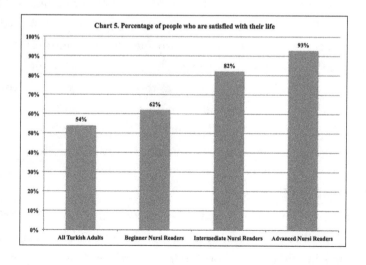

In terms of overall life satisfaction, the beginner Nursi readers fall in the high level of satisfaction while the intermediate and advanced groups fall in the highest level of life satisfaction. The mean score increases from 5.5 points to 6.3 when they advance in their reading level of Nursi. The increase of life satisfaction across the groups is consistent for all five questions. This is evidence that among Nursi readers, the more they engage with Nursi's writing, the more they increase their life satisfaction.

On the other hand, the intermediate group of Nursi readers falls into the highly satisfied category while the advanced group is just one-point shy of the extremely satisfied category based on the median score of 28.5. This means that the individuals in the advanced group "love their lives and feel that things are going very well. Their lives are not perfect, but they feel that things are about as good as lives get." The individuals in the intermediate group feel that things are mostly going well. Means comparison between the three groups, using one-way ANOVA, shows statistically significant values for each question related to SWB.

The need satisfaction scores indicate how much the respondents were satisfied with fulfilling their particular needs. The advanced Nursi readers score extremely high for spiritual, intellectual, conscience, aesthetics experience, social, altruistic, and emotional pleasures. Second, the satisfaction scores increased as the level of Nursi readers rose. In other words, the advanced group had greater satisfaction in need fulfillment for all needs except egoistic need. Indeed, other questions on egoistic goals and values clearly indicate that Nursi readers do not think favorably about egoistic pleasures. Therefore, the decline in the egoistic score when we moved from the beginner to the advanced group was consistent with other findings. Third, the highest mean gains between beginner and the advanced group were seen for the fulfillment of spiritual and intellectual needs followed by social, emotional, sensual, aesthetics experience needs.

Discussion of the Findings

Nursi places great importance on a spirituality based on a verified belief not set on blind imitation. For that, he insists on intensive involvement in reading and reflection in addition to worshipping. Therefore, it is not surprising to see spirituality as the most important life domain for Nursi readers. Second, Nursi mentions conscience, or what Freud refers to as the super-ego, as an important human psychological process that results in discomfort when we act unfairly and dishonestly. As an important part of their spiritual beliefs and study, Nursi readers place high importance on fairness and honesty in their lives. Third, the high scores for affiliation, intellectual life, and personal growth are consistent with the teachings of Nursi. Indeed, Nursi puts great emphasis on sincere friendship and family values. Nursi readers regularly come together for intellectual and spiritual activities. Fourth, the positive score for the aesthetic experience is reflected in Nursi's emphasis on the artistic dimension of God's works in the universe. Nursi urges his readers to observe the manifest beauty in the universe as a great sign of God's existence. Nursi readers focus on the beauty of the Universe and therefore regard aesthetic pleasure as important to their level of well-being. Fifth, the positive score for conformity may be due to Nursi's teaching of tolerance and universal friendship. Indeed, Nursi encourages his readers to feel a friendship with everything in the universe by understanding their interconnectedness as creatures of God. Sixth, the positive score for altruism might be a result of Nursi's emphasis on sacrifice as a required quality of sincere friendship and brotherhood/sisterhood.

The importance of Nursi's teaching can also explain the negative aspiration index scores. For Nursi readers, hedonism is least important or even most harmful to their level of happiness. Nursi provides compelling evidence against hedonic pleasures as a source of happiness. Nursi argues that hedonic pleasures contain poison; therefore, they result in painful rather than pure pleasures. In his view, the source of this type of pleasure is the instinctual soul. He encourages his readers to stay away from these types of pleasures (as a fulfillment of need). He provides spiritual and intellectual training for such restraint. The more people read the Nursi collection, the more they avoid hedonic pleasures. Second, the high negative scores for both popularity and image might be due to Nursi's emphasis on the egoistic self as the most dangerous internal enemy. Nursi argues that the understanding of God and submission to His power could happen only if we understand who we are and give up our imaginary egotism/godship. Third, the negative score for materialist values and money might reflect Nursi's emphasis on the worldly possessions as a means rather than an end goal. Even though Nursi acknowledges the importance of material gains as means, he warns his readers about indulging in material possession as an end goal. Finally, the negative score for the fear and insecurity might be due to Nursi's emphasis on the absolute control of God in all worldly affairs. Nursi argues that those who have certainty in God as the Absolute Power in control of everything with infinite mercy and absolute goodness would not worry about anything. They will do their part and place their trust in God.

Pleasure Pyramid of Those with Highest Happiness Score

Since the advanced Nursi readers seemed to achieve the highest happiness, it is important to present their rankings of pleasures. We would like to see what works for them by examining their pleasure pyramid. Based on the rating of pleasure among the advanced Nursi readers, we depicted the pleasure pyramid as seen in Chart 6. It is clear that the intellectual and emotional pleasures are the peak of the pyramid for advanced Nursi readers. This means that for the advanced Nursi readers, spirituality, intellectual growth, love and compassion are the most desired qualities in their lives. In other words, if they were asked to give the three most important keys for happiness, they would say: pray, read, and love. This is quite consistent with the teaching of Nursi. In Nursi's view, since the source of love is God, the love for worldly things is part of the love of God if one understands that his or her object of love is nothing other than the manifestation of the names of God.

According to the pleasure pyramid, the other secrets for happiness are hidden in the appreciation of the arts and beauty, in the honest and fair acts, in the altruistic behaviors, in the family and friendship, in the personal growth, and the enjoyment of sensual pleasures. Putting sensual pleasure at the bottom of the list does not mean that advanced Nursi readers do not enjoy sensual pleasures. Indeed, they read Nursi more as they experience sensual pleasures. However, compared to another type of pleasure, for the advanced Nursi readers, sensual pleasure is the least important.

Chart 6. The Pleasure Pyramid of for the Advanced Nursi Readers

Conclusion

Both of the studies discussed above provide compelling evidence for the importance of eudemonic and G-donic dimensions in pursuing higher happiness. The first study clearly shows that the hedonic dimension is relevant for short-term happiness, but does not help in the long-run. On the other hand, any improvement in the eudemonic and G-donic dimensions contributes to happiness in both short and long terms. However, the contribution is higher in the long-run. It is obvious that those who have a high score in both eudemonic and G-donic dimensions have the highest likelihood to experience the highest happiness.

The second study confirmed similar findings among the followers of Nursi. The study revealed that those participants that study, practice, and live according to the teachings of Nursi report great levels of satisfaction. The teachings of Nursi emphasize a life dedicated to God, love, compassion, service to others and high spiritual achievement and de-emphasize hedonic pleasures and materialism. Although it is not known if these teachings would result in the same findings across societies, cultures, and religions, the results suggest that the spiritual values taught by Nursi result in high levels of life satisfaction in practicing participants. The study makes it clear that a life filled with spiritual growth, positive emotions, psychology, and behaviors, and a desire to improve oneself and humanity contribute more to wellbeing and life satisfaction than a life dedicated to hedonic pleasures and materialism. The study shows that spirituality could offer path happiness for those who are trapped in the "hedonic treadmill" and the midlife crisis.

Indeed, while materialism attempts to fulfill the sensual desires of human beings through conspicuous consumption, Nursi offers a happiness model through moderate material consumption and spiritual nourishment. He also provides the means to control sensual desires. He thinks that it is necessary to be freed from material desires in order to develop our spiritual dimension. He believes that we are spiritual beings sent to this materialistic world to find and reach the Divine, not to live an animal form of life. Therefore, spiritual development is the essential goal for a practicing believer who is supposed to detach his/her heart from all material attachments and adhere to the Divine. In Nursi's view, although happiness is not life's purpose for a believer, it is the byproduct of his spiritual journey.

Chapter 16

Learned Lessons for a Happy Life

"God grant me the serenity to accept the things I cannot change, the courage to change the things I can, the wisdom to know the difference."
—The Serenity Prayer

Introduction

began my search for happiness in an extremely deprived condition. **It took three decades for me to move from the bottom one percent of the world population to the top one percent in terms of wealth and income.** The money gave me great opportunities to fulfill my dream of seeking pleasure and possession. I also managed to move from being a part-time shepherd to a full professor with two different doctoral degrees. However, I failed to find lasting satisfaction. I realized that my failure was due to my search for happiness through having, doing, and being in one dimension. Furthermore, I learned that happiness is not a destination; instead, it is a journey itself. Therefore, it is not possible to reach lasting happiness by pursuing pleasure, possession, or position within the hedonic (pleasure-seeking) dimension. In other words, pursuing the desires for pleasure, possession, power, and position (fame) will not bring lasting happiness even if we succeed in fulfilling them. We will sooner or later hit the DEAD loop and become dissatisfied and depressed. At that stage, the pursuit of meaning through the eudemonic (earthly meaning) dimension will help us to extend our happy journey. However, that will come to an end as well. We will never be satisfied with anything short of the realization of the ultimate reality and resetting our life objectives accordingly.

All is Vanity[15]

My search for happiness is not unique. Likewise, my conclusion is not unique either. Perhaps, my journey is just a modern version of the happiness story of the king of Jerusalem as told in Ecclesiastes 1-12 of the Old Testament. The King story begins with his conclusion, telling us that the search for happiness is a burden ordained by God to strive after the wind:

1. The words of the Preacher, the son of David, king in Jerusalem.
2. Vanity of vanities, says the Preacher, vanity of vanities! All is vanity.
3. What does man gain by all the toil at which he toils under the sun?
4. A generation goes, and a generation comes, but the earth remains forever.
5. The sun rises, and the sun goes down, and hastens to the place where it rises.
6. The wind blows to the south and goes around to the north; around and around goes the wind, and on its circuits the wind returns.
7. All streams run to the sea, but the sea is not full; to the place where the streams flow, there they flow again.
8. All things are full of weariness; a man cannot utter it; the eye is not satisfied with seeing, nor the ear filled with hearing.
9. What has been is what will be, and what has been done is what will be done, and there is nothing new under the sun.
10. Is there a thing of which it is said, "See, this is new"? It has been already in the ages before us.

---

15 Ecclesiastes 1-12 English Standard Version, https://www.biblegateway.com/passage/?search=Ecclesiastes+1-12&version=ESV, accessed on November 25, 2018.

11. There is no remembrance of former things, nor will there be any remembrance of later things yet to be among those who come after.

12. I the Preacher have been king over Israel in Jerusalem.

13. And I applied my heart to seek and to search out by wisdom all that is done under heaven. It is an unhappy business that God has given to the children of man to be busy with.

14. I have seen everything that is done under the sun, and behold, all is vanity and a striving after wind.

The Vanity of Self-Indulgence

Then, the unhappy king details his failed journey to find happiness. He speaks of vanity in pursuing hedonic happiness through having, doing, and being.

15. I said in my heart, "Come now, I will test you with pleasure; enjoy yourself." But behold, this also was vanity.

16. I said of laughter, "It is mad," and of pleasure, "What use is it?"

17. I searched with my heart how to cheer my body with wine—my heart still guiding me with wisdom—and how to lay hold on folly, till I might see what was good for the children of man to do under heaven during the few days of their life.

18. I made great works. I built houses and planted vineyards for myself.

19. I made myself gardens and parks, and planted in them all kinds of fruit trees.

20. I made myself pools from which to water the forest of growing trees.

21. I bought male and female slaves, and had slaves who were born in my house. I had also great possessions of herds and flocks, more than any who had been before me in Jerusalem.

22. I also gathered for myself silver and gold and the treasure of kings and provinces. I got singers, both men and women, and many concubines, the delight of the sons of man.

23. So, I became great and surpassed all who were before me in Jerusalem. Also, my wisdom remained with me.

24. And whatever my eyes desired I did not keep from them. I kept my heart from no pleasure, for my heart found pleasure in all my toil, and this was my reward for all my toil.

25. Then I considered all that my hands had done and the toil I had expended in doing it, and behold, all was vanity and a striving after wind, and there was nothing to be gained under the sun.

The Vanity of Living Wisely

The king then turned to wisdom in his search for happiness. Basically, he moved to the eudemonic dimension after hitting the dead end in the hedonic dimension. However, he could not find happiness in wisdom either because he realized that the ultimate end is no different for the fool and the wise.

26. So, I turned to consider wisdom and madness and folly. For what can the man do who comes after the king? Only what has already been done.

27. Then I saw that there is more gain in wisdom than in folly, as there is more gain in light than in darkness.

28. The wise person has his eyes in his head, but the fool walks in darkness. And yet I perceived that the same event happens to all of them.

29. Then I said in my heart, "What happens to the fool will happen to me also. Why then have I been so very wise?" And I said in my heart that this also is vanity.

30. For of the wise as of the fool there is no enduring remembrance, seeing that in the days to come all will have been long forgotten. How the wise dies just like the fool!

31. So, I hated life, because what is done under the sun was grievous to me, for all is vanity and a striving after wind.

The Happy end with God

The preacher king came to the realization that his failure was due to the desire for eternity which could not be satisfied with anything but God.

32. I have seen the business that God has given to the children of man to be busy with.

33. He has made everything beautiful in its time. Also, he has put eternity into man's heart, yet so that he cannot find out what God has done from the beginning to the end.

34. I perceived that there is nothing better for them than to be joyful and to do good as long as they live; also, that everyone should eat and drink and take pleasure in all his toil—this is God's gift to man.

35. I perceived that whatever God does endures forever; nothing can be added to it, nor anything taken from it. God has done it, so that people fear before him.

Finding Higher Happiness in Higher Dimensions

Indeed, the King is right, we cannot find satisfaction in striving after the wind. A similar message is found in other religious and spiritual books as well. For instance, the Quran, the holy book of Muslims, describes the vanity in human life as follows:

"KNOW [O men] that the life of this world is but a play and a passing delight, and a beautiful show, and [the cause of] your boastful vying with one another, and [of your] greed for more and more riches and children. Its parable is that of [life-giving] rain: the herbage which it causes to grow delights the tillers of the soil; but then it withers, and you can see it turn yellow; and in the end it crumbles into dust...for the life of this world is nothing but an enjoyment of self-delusion." (Al-Hadid, 57:20)

It does not matter how successful we become in accumulating our possession of shadow-like wealth and titles through having, doing, and being, we will not be satisfied. Even if we assign meaning to our endeavors, we cannot avoid the ultimate meaningless in everything. We cannot be satisfied with anything short of eternity. Everything eventually will crumble into dust as we are heading to unavoidable death. Thus, it is necessary to go beyond hedonic and eudemonic dimensions and search for the ultimate reality and meaning for lasting satisfaction. This is what we call the G-donic (transcendental and spiritual meaning) dimension.

We argue that neither money, nor science and technology can help us to find authentic happiness. It is true that science has enabled us to gain instrumental knowledge to improve our material wellbeing. However, it offers nothing to quench our innate thirst for the ultimate reality and transcendental meaning. Indeed, as elegantly described by Bertrand Russell, a British philosopher, mathematician, historian and Nobel laureate, modern science makes everything ultimately meaningless:

"Such, in outline, but even more purposeless, more void of meaning, is the world which Science presents for our belief. Amid such a world, if anywhere, our ideals henceforward must find a home. That man is the product of causes which had no prevision of the end they were achieving; that his origin, his growth, his hopes and fears, his loves and his beliefs, are but the outcome of accidental collocations of atoms; that no fire, no heroism, no intensity of thought and feeling, can preserve an individual life beyond the grave; that all the labors of the ages, all the devotion, all the inspiration, all the noonday brightness of human genius, are destined to extinction in the vast death of the solar system, and that the whole temple of man's achievement must inevitably be buried beneath the debris of a universe in ruins—all these things, if not quite beyond dispute, are yet so nearly certain that no philosophy that rejects them can hope to stand…"[16]

It does not matter how successful we are in the accumulation of having, doing, being, and temporal meaning, they are all doomed to be thrown into the garbage of the solar system. That is what science tells us for sure. In other words, one day, the sun will run out of its limited fuel of hydrogen and stop giving us the necessary light and power. Thus, the earth and everything within will perish. Therefore, we have to face the existential question raised by Russell in the same article above: "How in such an alien and inhuman world, can so powerless a creature as man preserve his aspirations untarnished?" We argue that the solution lies in the G-donic dimension. Indeed, we can define the expected outcome equation for humanity as follows:

Expected life outcome = payoff X probability of keeping for eternity

16   Bertrand Russell, "A Free Man's Worship," 1903

If there is zero probability for eternity, then, everything is ultimately zero. If there is no God as secular science suggests, that is what we will get. However, if there is God, the expected outcome will be infinite as long as the probability of God's existence is greater than zero.

Of course, our belief in God should not be based on our wish for eternity. That would be self-deception. It should be based on compelling evidence. God with the right attributes will be sufficient for lasting happiness in this world and beyond. As we see the signs of God's attributes as All-Good, All-Powerful, All-Knowing, Most-Merciful, Most-Kind, we will know that God is sufficient to overcome our obstacles and fulfill our needs and desires that last to eternity. We will also realize that as long as we do not choose to make something bad for ourselves, everything is either directly or by consequences good, since they all are the choices of the All-Good God. The painful suffering in life would be endured because we will find meaning in it. In this regard, painful experiences might be more rewarding than the pleasant ones. We will perceive almost infinite bounties granted to us from moment to moment. By realizing how we benefit from everything in the universe, regardless of what we accumulate through our works, we will know that we have already received infinite gifts. We will be thankful for what we have now and hopeful for what we will have for eternity.

Higher Pleasure as a Byproduct of Higher Dimensions

The G-donic model does not suggest a form of ascetic life in terms of abstaining from worldly pleasure. Rather, it provides a way of gaining even higher sensual pleasure through exploring higher dimensions. Thus, our argument is that, once you gain insight about the ultimate meaning in life through the G-donic model, you will get even higher pleasure as a byproduct of your expanded perspective. In other words, we argue that higher happiness with having, doing, and being is positively correlated to the higher dimensions of happiness. For instance, you could have a different experience from eating, picnicking, and vacationing depending on the dimension in which you pursue happiness.

Increasing Satisfaction from Eating

In the hedonic dimension, the purpose is to be happy through maximizing sensual pleasure from eating. Thus, eating is not just fuel for the body; it is an essential means of pleasure. We will seek the best restaurants and try the best meals to experience the higher pleasure of eating. We will feel unhappy if we do not have the opportunity to eat enjoyable food. In the eudemonic dimension, our primary goal is not pleasure maximization, but meaning maximization. We value food as fuel to help us to get something meaningful in life. Therefore, we do not necessarily look for the best food to be happy in life. Of course, we could still eat good food and experience immense sensual pleasure. However, even if we eat at the best restaurant in the world, we could not be satisfied if we do not have a meaningful outcome in our daily life. On the other hand, we can still be happy if we manage to produce a meaningful outcome but fail to enjoy great food.

In the G-donic dimension, similar to the eudemonic dimension, our aim is not to maximize pleasure through eating the best food. Instead, our objective is to realize the transcendental reality. Thus, food is not just fuel for the body; it is also food for the mind in terms of being a meaningful sign of transcendental reality. It is like a coded message. As we eat food, we will try to read its coded message about the transcendental reality. For instance, while making apple pie, we will try to understand how a ready-made dessert such as an apple came into existence. We make apple pie by combining certain ingredients at a certain measure. We know a stone sculpture cannot make an apple pie because it does not have the necessary power and knowledge to put ingredients together in a precise measure. A monkey cannot make it either because he/she has power, but not sufficient knowledge. Thus, we know with certainty that it takes conscience, knowledge, power, and will to make an apple pie.

Then, we can apply the same reasoning to understand an apple which a dessert-like fruit is. It is a much healthier one. Like apple pie, an apple is nothing but a mix of certain ingredients that are no secret to us. At the macro level, we see an apple is composed out of the soil, animal waste (fertilizer), water, and the sun power. Nothing else. We know that if we give water, soil, and animal waste to the best chef in the world, he cannot make an apple because he does not have enough power and knowledge to convert those ingredients into the desert. At the micro level, even if we ask all the scientists around the world to work on ingredients of an apple at the nano level and compose an apple from them, they still could not do that. Simply it is because they do not have enough power and knowledge to construct the given ingredients into an apple.

Thus, an apple is not just food; it is a message about the Infinite Power. It is a book describing the attribute of its Maker. As we read this charming book, we learn that its Maker must be All-Powerful, All-Knowing, All-Wise, Most-Merciful, and Most-Kind to make such an extraordinary dessert for us. He makes an apple, He must be the Maker of everything else, given the fact that everything is no different from an apple in terms of its complexity. He must be the Maker of our body and universe as well. For sure, the One who creates us and the universe out of nothing can give us eternal life. Thus, we shall seek His Mercy and Kindness through our realization of the apple. It is He behind this phenomenal reality of the apple and the universe. We shall seek Him for eternal satisfaction, not a temporal reflection of His reality in this transient world.

Increasing Satisfaction from Picnicking

We argue that having a picnic at a nice park brings a different level of satisfaction depending on our happiness model. At the hedonic level, the purpose of a picnic is to maximize pleasure. Thus, we have to have delicious food and organize great fun activities to be happy at the picnic. We have to ignore existential questions to enjoy our picnic. We have to try different locations and food to overcome diminishing marginal utility from repeating the same experience. It does not matter what we do; we cannot avoid the ultimate disappointment with picnicking.

At the eudemonic level, the picnic will be desirable only if it helps us to be more productive in our objective of meaning maximization. In other words, we could enjoy a picnic if it will help us to relax and perform better the next day when we try to accomplish a meaningful goal. Even if we have the most pleasant picnic, if that prevents us from achieving a meaningful goal, it will be worthless. Thus, we value the picnic only if it helps as a means to achieve our end of meaning maximization.

In the G-donic dimension, a picnic is neither an opportunity for pleasure maximization nor a means for meaningful accomplishment; it is an opportunity to explore a more transcendental reality. Unlike in the hedonic dimension, we are not interested in taking a picture and sharing it on social media such as Facebook to brag about it. We will be happy if we transcend the observed phenomena and remember the ultimate reality behind it. Thus, we see the nice scene as a meaningful book. We should try to read the transcendental meaning of this book. It would be childish to waste time taking a picture but not trying to read and understand the exciting message in this book. For instance, when we look at a tree, we will read it by trying to reflect on its transcendental reality. As we understand its apparent and inner elegance, we will have a higher awareness of its Maker as All-Powerful, All-Knowing, All-Wise, Most-Merciful, and Most-Kind. We will feel that the entire existence comes from this Hidden Power. As long as He is All-Powerful and Everlasting, our existence will be eternal, too. That is because our existence is like a shadowy reflection of His existence. As long as the Origin persists, the shadow will persist, also.

Increasing Satisfaction from Vacationing

We argue that our satisfaction from vacation depends on the happiness dimensions in which we live. In the hedonic dimension, the objective is to maximize utility through various fun activities. Since we care about our perception in the eyes of others, we will try to go to places with high status. We feel that we will be happier if we go to well-known destinations and stay at luxury hotels. We almost focus entirely on sensual and egoistic pleasure to reach higher satisfaction.

In the eudemonic dimension, we will plan our vacation to gain sensual and intellectual pleasure. We will use the vacation as a retreat to be recharged for a flourishing life. Thus, we do not have to stay in expensive hotels or go to well-known destinations. Our goal is neither maximization of sensual pleasure nor boosting our ego by sharing our vacation pictures. We will be content with any place that helps to relax and recharge for higher accomplishments. We will enjoy visiting places to expand our knowledge of nature, culture, countries, etc.

In the G-donic dimension, our objective is neither pleasure maximization nor accomplishment. We will use vacation to retreat from our busy daily life to reflect on transcendental meaning. It is time to reflect on existential questions and explore the deep transcendental meaning of the observed phenomena. It is not necessary to go to luxury destinations. Indeed, we will try to stay away from common destinations. We will prefer to stay close to nature. We will feel much more satisfied if the vacation helps us to penetrate deep into the transcendental meaning of life. Though we might have relaxing fun activities and enjoy eating delicious food, they are not the primary goals.

Twelve Principles for higher happiness

I would like to end the book with memorable principles for a happy and heroic life. As Buddha says, the real hero is the one who overcomes his internal enemies and gains his true freedom, not the one who defeats external enemies: "A man who conquers himself is greater than one who conquers a thousand men in battle." We argue that it is necessary to engage in heroic wars with the carnal desires that pursue pleasure and possession, the inner showman (ego) that pursues fame, and the will to power that pursues command and control.

Perhaps, as Nietzsche argued, we need to go through a three-staged metamorphosis: camel, lion, and child. In other words, we need to move from the hedonic toward the eudemonic and G-donic dimensions to have a happy and fulfilled life. In the first stage, like a camel, we just follow the herd in fulfilling the desires for pleasure, possession, and power that are imposed on us by consumer culture. In the second stage, like a lion, we gain the courage to go against the current by questioning the meaning of what we are doing and pursuing higher goals. In the third stage, like a child, we begin perceiving the bewildering and meaningful lessons in everything. We argue that happiness is the outcome of such freedom, courage, and wisdom in living your life based on the following twelve principles:

Freedom from pleasure, possession, people, and power

1. You shall gain freedom from sensual **PLEASURE** rather than being the slave of your desires.
2. You shall gain freedom from **POSSESSION** of things rather than following the crazy consumer culture.

3. You shall gain freedom from **PEOPLE** rather than seeking fame and approval of others.

4. You shall gain freedom from seeking **POWER** rather than following the self-deceptive and self-destructive will to power.

Courage for authenticity, nothingness, mortality, and eternity

5. You shall have the courage to develop the **AUTHENTIC self** (be yourself) rather than having a fake self.

6. You shall have the courage to accept **NOTHINGNESS** as the final outcome of our worldly efforts if there is no eternity.

7. You shall have the courage to accept your **MORTALITY** as the most certain reality of life.

8. You shall have the courage to **VENTURE** to higher dimensions for the ultimate meaning and eternity.

Wisdom to know, read, realize, and redefine

9. You shall gain the wisdom to **KNOW** that life is nothing but a journey to learn the unfolding meaning behind everything

10. You shall gain the wisdom to **READ** the meaningful lessons in both pleasant and painful life experiences

11. You shall gain the wisdom to **REALIZE** that your very existence means that you are receiving an infinite number of infinitely valuable gifts from moment to moment.

12. You shall gain the wisdom to **REDEFINE** your happiness function as the realization of the principles above for you and others in all life experiences.

Measure Three Dimensions of Your Happiness

First Dimension: Hedonic Happiness Scale

Please answer six questions below, then add up your score for each item to calculate your total hedonic score. For the meaning of your score, please check the guiding information at the end of this section.

I enjoy watching entertainment media on platforms such as YouTube, TV, etc.	Score
o Never	1
o Very rarely	2
o Rarely	3
o Occasionally	4
o Frequently	5
o Very frequently	6
I seek pleasure through luxury consumption if I could afford it.	
o Never	1
o Very rarely	2

o	Rarely	3
o	Occasionally	4
o	Frequently	5
o	Very frequently	6

I agree with the phrase "money buys happiness".

o	Strongly disagree	1
o	Moderately disagree	2
o	Slightly disagree	3
o	Slightly agree	4
o	Moderately agree	5
o	Strongly agree	6

I impress others through my possession and position.

o	Never	1
o	Very rarely	2
o	Rarely	3
o	Occasionally	4
o	Frequently	5
o	Very frequently	6

The phrase "life is fun," summarizes my life philosophy.

o	Strongly disagree	1
o	Moderately disagree	2
o	Slightly disagree	3
o	Slightly agree	4
o	Moderately agree	5
o	Strongly agree	6

It is important for me to keep up with fashion if I can afford it.

o	Strongly disagree	1
o	Moderately disagree	2
o	Slightly disagree	3
o	Slightly agree	4
o	Moderately agree	5

o Strongly agree	6
Total Hedonic Score	

Second Dimension: Eudemonic Happiness Scale

Please answer six questions below, then add up your score for each item to calculate your total eudemonic score. For the meaning of your score, please check the guiding information at the end of this section.

I seek out situations that challenge my skills and abilities.	Score
o Strongly agree	1
o Moderately agree	2
o Slightly agree	3
o Slightly disagree	4
o Moderately disagree	5
o Strongly disagree	6
My life is centered around a set of core beliefs that give meaning to my life.	
o Strongly agree	1
o Moderately agree	2
o Slightly agree	3
o Slightly disagree	4
o Moderately disagree	5
o Strongly disagree	6
It is more important that I genuinely enjoy what I do rather than focus on whether other people are impressed by it.	
o Strongly agree	1
o Moderately agree	2
o Slightly agree	3
o Slightly disagree	4
o Moderately disagree	5
o Strongly disagree	6
I can say that I have found my purpose in life.	

o	Strongly agree	o	1
o	Moderately agree	o	2
o	Slightly agree	o	3
o	Slightly disagree	o	4
o	Moderately disagree	o	5
o	Strongly disagree	o	6
When I engage in activities that involve my best potentials, I have a sense of truly being alive.			
o	Strongly agree	o	1
o	Moderately agree	o	2
o	Slightly agree	o	3
o	Slightly disagree	o	4
o	Moderately disagree	o	5
o	Strongly disagree	o	6
It is important to me that I feel fulfilled by the activities I engage in.			
o	Strongly agree	o	1
o	Moderately agree	o	2
o	Slightly agree	o	3
o	Slightly disagree	o	4
o	Moderately disagree	o	5
o	Strongly disagree	o	6
Your Total Eudemonic Score			

Third Dimension: G-donic Happiness Scale

Please answer six questions below, then add up your score for each item to calculate your total G-donic score. For the meaning of your score, please check the guiding information at the end of this section.

I believe in:	Score
o No God whatsoever.	1
o God's existence with serious doubt	2

o	God who created the universe with specific laws and DOES NOT intervene beyond that.	3
o	God who created the universe with specific laws and EXCEPTIONALLY intervenes in natural events.	4
o	God who created the universe with specific laws and ALWAYS intervenes in natural events.	5
o	God who created the universe with specific laws and DIRECTLY intervenes in natural events AND my life events.	6
I feel God's presence as if I see Him.		
o	Never	1
o	Very rarely	2
o	Rarely	3
o	Occasionally	4
o	Frequently	5
o	Very frequently	6
I experience the highest level of satisfaction by having a strong relationship with God.		
o	Never	1
o	Very rarely	2
o	Rarely	3
o	Occasionally	4
o	Frequently	5
o	Very frequently	6
I believe my prayers are answered by God one way or another.		
o	Strongly disagree	1
o	Moderately disagree	2
o	Slightly disagree	3
o	Slightly agree	4
o	Moderately agree	5

o Strongly agree	6
I worship God.	
o Never	1
o Few times in a year	2
o Few times in a month	3
o Few times in a week	4
o One or two times a day.	5
o Few times in a day	6
I believe that my life continues after death.	
o Do not believe at all	1
o Slightly believe with serious doubt	2
o Moderately believe with some doubt	3
o Moderately believe with no doubt	4
o Strongly believe with some doubt	5
o Strongly believe with no doubt	6
Your total G-donic score	

Guideline on the Meaning of Your Score

Once you calculate your dimension score, you can use the table below to learn your level for each dimension. If you want to compare your score with the mean score of others who did participate in the 3D of happiness survey, please visit www.3dhappiness.org

Hedonic Dimension Score	Level	Eudemonic Dimension Score	Level	G-donic Dimension Score	Level
30-36	High	30-36	High	30-36	High
18-29	Moderate	18-29	Moderate	18-29	Moderate
6-17	Low	6-17	Low	6-17	Low

Twelve Books for Higher Dimensions of Happiness

have read more than three thousand books in my life. I put them into three categories in terms of their significance to me: 1) The junk books that I regret having read, 2) The fine books that are worth reading once, 3) The good books that are worthy of reading twice or more. Hereby, I would like to share my thirteen favorite books in reverse order out of three thousand books. I think they will help in moving to higher dimensions of happiness.

12. *A Secular Age* by Charles Taylor

The book provides compelling evidence for secularization of mind and life in terms of pursuing a largely hedonic happiness model. The book helps to understand how our minds have been shaped through secular ideology since the enlightenment and how, in reality, everyone including most religious/spiritual people pursue hedonic or eudemonic happiness even if they claim that they pursue G-donic happiness.

11. Animal Farm by George Orwell

The book provides an excellent account revealing how people pursue the will to power by disguising their true intention until they gain power. The book helps to see the true face of those who fight to gain power under various disguises. After reading this book, you might lose your belief in anyone who makes promises for positive changes through acquiring power. This is a satirical book. If you want to read deep intellectual books with the same type of message, I recommend *The Prince* by Machiavelli and *The Will to Power* by Nietzsche.

10. A Theory of Justice by John Rawls

The book provides excellent justification for justice. Through logical arguments, the book defines justice and makes very compelling arguments for why we all need justice. After reading this book, justice became a supreme value for me for which I think it is worth sacrificing everything, including my life if necessary. The book convinces readers that they should pursue higher pleasure by pursuing justice, even if that will mean losing some sensual and egoistic pleasures that will come through unjust gains.

9. The Language of God by Francis S. Collins

The book provides an amazing intellectual and spiritual journey of the author who led the team to count human genes for the first time. The author was raised as a Christian. He lost his faith once he discovered inconsistency between his faith and science as he went through his college education. He had to come back to God again as he studied genes and reflected on the deep meaning behind the amazing coding in living beings. The book helps to view living beings as elegant books written by God, not accidental chemical soup as claimed by atheist scientists.

8. Elegant Universe by Brian Greene

The book provides a great perspective in terms of how to perceive material reality through the lens of quantum physics. It helps to understand that the subatomic system is even more elegant than the galactical system with billions of stars. After reading this book, I came to realize that we live in a truly elegant universe in which one small component of its fabric is as well-designed as the entire universe. A PBS documentary with the same name helps to further digest the ideas in this book through simulation and visual presentation of the ideas discussed.

7. *The Tao of Physics* by Fritjof Capra

The book shows how science and religion meet at the peak of their journey to an understanding of the truth. It shows how with quantum physics, scientists revealed an image of reality that has been preached by many religious figures for centuries. In a sense that, as scientists reached the top of the mountain of truth, they were surprised to find that some spiritual and religious people have been waiting there for centuries. The book convinces readers that real science and authentic spirituality might actually complement each other rather than compete with each other. Even if you disagree that Taoism is the best way to explain the modern scientific mystery, you would love a bit of religious and mystical perspective that helps scientists to make better sense of what they have discovered in recent decades.

6. *Confession* by Tolstoy

The book is a true confession of the author who was born into a wealthy family and experimented with all kinds of sensual pleasure until he came to realize that it was all vanity. Then, he embarked on meaningful activities: raising his biological kids through family life and producing intellectual offspring through authorship. However, he eventually came to the same conclusion, realizing that meaningful worldly activities are also meaningless at the end. He explored an authentic spiritual path to find transcendental meaning. The book helps to unmask those who claim to be happy through sensual pleasure (hedonism) and worldly accomplishment (eudemonism). It inspired me to write this book as my own confession.

5. *Denial of Death* by Ernest Becker

This book is undoubtedly the best book on the reality of death. The author claims that as soon as we become aware of our mortality, we indulge in all kinds of activities to deny the unavoidable reality of death. He provides much compelling evidence for its core argument, showing how we try to deny this obvious fact. It argues that we should consider the desire for eternity and denial of mortality as the driving force behind our choices, not our sexual drive as argued by Freud. Ironically, the author himself died just six months after publishing this book, confirming the reality of death through his own journey. The book convinces readers that it is useless deception to ignore the reality of death, which exists for humans only as a phenomenal conscious experience. The author argues that we can never reach lasting happiness if we do not find a way to cope with this painful possibility that will end all possibilities.

4. *Thus Spoke Zarathustra* by Friedrich Nietzsche

Though Nietzsche was famous for his declaration that "God is dead", in my view, he wanted God to be alive more than anyone. He recognized how life without God would be ultimately meaningless. However, he had no choice but to deny the Christian God because it did not make any sense to him. Indeed, he claimed that it was Christian priests who killed their god through making the religion as nothing but a means for their power and benefits. For Nietzsche, the denial of God was not an excuse to embrace the decadent culture. In this book, Nietzsche strongly argued the uselessness of decadent culture in pursuit of little pleasure. Instead, he preached some transcendent meaning through his ideal figure of Ubermensch. Through his personal life and elegant writings, Nietzsche helps readers to pursue higher dimensions rather than being stuck in a sensual and egoistic treadmill. As we discussed in one chapter in this book, Nietzsche is a real guide to diagnose mortal diseases of modern society.

3. *Being and Time* by Heidegger

This is one of the best books ever written for those who read and digest its difficult but extremely enriching message. The inspiring question for Heidegger for this very complicated book is an apparently easy question: what is IS? Heidegger argues that nothing is more important than this forgotten question. He encourages readers to reflect on being as unfolding meaning to the conscious. The book changed my view forever in terms of perceiving beings as meaningful statements rather than instruments. It particularly helped me to reflect on my own being for whom being does matter. It makes a compelling argument that what matters is meaning, which only exists for the conscious.

2. *Nicomachean Ethics* by Aristotle

Aristotle, who inherited deep intellectual discourse from Plato (his teacher) and Socrates (his teacher's teacher), wrote this book for his son as a guide for a happy and fulfilled life. In my view, the book could be considered the first scientific book on human life. It follows a very systematic and analytical method in defining a path for happiness. As we discussed earlier, this book set the foundation for eudemonic happiness. I particularly like the book for its elegant scientific approach to happiness and compelling logical arguments. It provides a great example of how to approach happiness through analytical and critical thinking.

1. *The Words* by Said Nursi

I came across the writings of Said Nursi in my first year of high school. For sure, he has been my lifetime mentor since then. It is not easy to understand his views because one needs to read his entire books which run to 6000 pages. I remember that I used to read 400 pages of his books per day to gain a holistic view of his ideas. After reading all of his books, he became my all-time favorite author. I consider his writings as main references for my personal and intellectual journey. I still read his books on a regular basis. It is not an accident that most of my academic articles are inspired by his ideas. For me, Nursi is an intellectual and spiritual master who managed to live a very happy life even in the most deprived conditions. In my imaginary intellectual coffee shop, Nursi sits shoulder-to-shoulder with the great minds mentioned above in search of a meaningful and fulfilled life[17]. To me, the influence of Nursi comes from the consistency between his writing and life. He was sincerely practicing whatever he was preaching.

---

17 If you want to read more about how Nursi offers a unifying perspective to integrate pure science and authentic spirituality, please refer to my following book: *Said Nursi and Science in Islam, Character Building through Nursi's mana-i harfi,* Routledge Press (May 2019).

About the Author

Dr.Necati Aydin currently works as a full professor of economics at Alfaisal University. He was the founding director of the Neuroeconomics and Well-being Program at Florida State University. The program was established to conduct well-being studies both at individual and societal levels, bringing experts from different subject areas together for qualitative and quantitative analysis on happiness related issues. Dr.Aydin has two doctoral degrees, one in Education and the other in Economics. He worked as a researcher for a decade, completing over forty research projects before embarking on his academic career. He has authored seven books, translated two, co-authored three books, and published many peer-reviewed articles. He recently published the following book with Routledge: *Said Nursi and Science in Islam, Character Building through Nursi's Mana-i harfi.*

Dr.Aydin currently focuses on the economics of wellbeing, human development, and neuroeconomics. His articles have been published in top academic journals including the Journal of Business Ethics, the International Journal of Social Economics, Humanomics and the Journal of Developing Areas. He is a referee for several academic journals including the Journal of Happiness Studies and the Journal of Applied Research in Quality of Life. He works on a project with a professor from Brown University to test three dimensions of happiness using functional MRI. He also conducts inter-disciplinary studies to explore empirical evidence for 3D happiness. For more information about his research activities, please visit www.3Dhappiness.org.

Bibliography

Abbott, Edwin Abbott. 1963. *Flatland : A Romance of Many Dimensions*. New York, N.Y., U.S.A.: Barnes & Noble.

Anić, Petra, and Marko Tončić. 2013. "Orientations to Happiness, Subjective Well-Being and Life Goals." *Psihologijske Teme* 22 (1). University of Rijeka: 135–53.

Aydin, N. 2012. "A Grand Theory of Human Nature and Happiness." *Humanomics* 28 (1).

———. 2013. "Seeking Self-Worth through Commodity Narcissism & Commodity Nihilism in the Light of Secular and Tawhidi Paradigms." *Al-Shajarah* 18 (2).

———. 2017. "Psycho-Economic Aspiration and Subjective Well-Being: Evidence from a Representative Turkish Sample." *International Journal of Social Economics* 44 (6).

Aydin, N., and E. Manusov. 2014. "Materialism, Hedonism, Spirituality, and Subjective Well-Being: An Empirical Study of Risale-I Nur (RN) Readers." *Al-Shajarah* 19 (2).

B, Duriez, Vansteenkiste M, Soenens B, and De Witte H. 2006. "Evidence for the Social Costs of Extrinsic Relative to Intrinsic Goal Pursuits: Their Relation with Right-Wing Authoritarianism, Social Dominance, and Prejudice." *Journal of Applied Social Psychology* 36 (12): 2892–2908.

Banerjee, Robin, and Helga Dittmar. 2008. "Individual Differences in
Children's Materialism: The Role of Peer Relations." *Personality & Social
Psychology Bulletin* 34 (1): 17–31.

Baumeister, R F, and M R Leary. 1995. "The Need to Belong: Desire for
Interpersonal Attachments as a Fundamental Human Motivation."
Psychological Bulletin 117 (3): 497–529.

Boes, Stefan, and Rainer Winkelmann. 2010. "The Effect of Income on
General Life Satisfaction and Dissatisfaction." *Social Indicators Research* 95
(1): 111–28.

Burroughs, James E., and Aric Rindfleisch. 2002. "Materialism and Well-
Being: A Conflicting Values Perspective." *Journal of Consumer Research* 29
(3): 348–70.

Cummins, B, E Gullone, and L A Lau. 2002. "A Model of Subjective Well-
Being Homeostasis: The Role of Personality." In , edited by E Gullone and
R A Cummins, 7–46. The Universality of Subjective Well-Being Indicators.
Netherlands: Kluwer.

DeCharms, Richard. 1968. *Personal Causation; the Internal Affective
Determinants of Behavior.* Academic Press. https://adams.marmot.org/
Record/.b17197478.

Deci, Edward L, and Richard M Ryan. 2000. "The 'What' and 'Why' of
Goal Pursuits: Human Needs and the Self-Determination of Behavior."
Psychological Inquiry 11 (4): 227.

Diener, Ed, Robert A Emmons, Randy J Larsen, and Sharon Griffin. 1985.
"The Satisfaction With Life Scale." *Journal of Personality Assessment* 49 (1):
71.

Dittmar, Helga., and Emma. Halliwell. 2008. *Consumer Culture, Identity
and Well-Being : The Search for the Good Life; and the Body Perfect;* Hove
[England] ;;New York: Psychology Press.

Dittmar, Helga, Rod Bond, Megan Hurst, and Tim Kasser. 2014. "The
Relationship between Materialism and Personal Well-Being: A Meta-
Analysis." *Journal of Personality and Social Psychology* 107 (5): 879–924.

Easterlin, Richard A. 1974. "Does Economic Growth Improve the Human
Lot?" In , edited by Moses Abramovitz, Paul A David, and Melvin W

Reder. Nations and Households in Economic Growth: Essays in Honor of Moses Abramovitz. New York: Academic Press.

Eastman, Jacqueline K., Ronald E. Goldsmith, and Leisa Reinecke Flynn. 1999. "Status Consumption in Consumer Behavior: Scale Development and Validation." *Journal of Marketing Theory and Practice* 7 (3). Routledge: 41–52.

Fromm, Erich. 1976. *To Have or to Be?* 1st ed. New York: Harper & Row.

Heaney, Joo-Gim, Ronald E. Goldsmith, and Wan Jamaliah Wan Jusoh. 2005. "Status Consumption Among Malaysian Consumers." *Journal of International Consumer Marketing* 17 (4). Taylor & Francis Group : 83–98.

Kashdan, Todd B. 2004. "The Assessment of Subjective Well-Being (Issues Raised by the Oxford Happiness Questionnaire)." *Personality and Individual Differences* 36 (5). Pergamon: 1225–32.

Kasser, Tim. 2002. *The High Price of Materialism*. Cambridge, Mass.: MIT Press.

———. 2008. "Pain and Insecurity, Love and Money." *Psychological Inquiry* 19 (3): 174–78.

Kasser, Tim, Steve Cohn, Allen D Kanner, and Richard M Ryan. 2007. "TARGET ARTICLE: Some Costs of American Corporate Capitalism: A Psychological Exploration of Value and Goal Conflicts." *Psychological Inquiry* 18 (1): 1–22.

Kasser, Tim, and Richard M Ryan. 1996. "Further Examining the American Dream: Differential Correlates of Intrinsic and Extrinsic Goals." *Personality & Social Psychology Bulletin.* 22 (3): 280.

———. 2001. "Be Careful What You Wish for: Optimal Functioning and the Relative Attainment of Intrinsic and Extrinsic Goals." In *Life Goals and Well-Being: Towards a Positive Psychology of Human Striving.*, 116–31. Ashland, OH, US: Hogrefe & Huber Publishers.

Klein, Naomi. 2001. *No Logo*. London: Flamingo.

McCracken, Grant. 1988. *Culture and Consumption*. Indiana University Press.

Niemiec, Christopher P, Richard M Ryan, and Edward L Deci. 2009. "The Path Taken: Consequences of Attaining Intrinsic and Extrinsic Aspirations in Post-College Life." *Journal of Research in Personality* 43 (3): 291–306.

Nietzsche, Friedrich. 2007. *Thus Spoke Zarathustra (Barnes & Noble Classics Series)*. Barnes & Noble.

Nietzsche, Friedrich Wilhelm, Michael A. Scarpitti, and R. Kevin Hill. 2012. *The Will to Power : Selections from the Notebooks of the 1880s*. Vintage Books.

Nursi, Said. 1996. *The Words*. Sozler Publications. www.erisale.org.

Pearce, David. 2015. *The Hedonistic Imperative*. Kindle. Amazon.

Peterson, Christopher, Nansook Park, and Martin E. P. Seligman. 2005. "Orientations to Happiness and Life Satisfaction: The Full Life versus the Empty Life." *Journal of Happiness Studies* 6 (1). Kluwer Academic Publishers: 25–41.

Richins, Marsha L., and Scott Dawson. 1992. "A Consumer Calues Orientation for Materialism and Its Measurement: Scale Development and Validation." *Journal of Consumer Research* 19 (3): 303–16.

Ryan, R. M., V. I. Chirkov, T. D. Little, K. M. Sheldon, E. Timoshina, and E. L. Deci. 1999. "The American Dream in Russia: Extrinsic Aspirations and Well-Being in Two Cultures." *Personality and Social Psychology Bulletin* 25 (12): 1509–24.

Sheldon, Kennon M., Richard M. Ryan, Edward L. Deci, and Tim Kasser. 2004. "The Independent Effects of Goal Contents and Motives on Well-Being: It's Both What You Pursue and Why You Pursue It." *Personality and Social Psychology Bulletin* 30 (4). SAGE Publications: 475–86.

Sirgy, M. Joseph. 2012. *The Psychology of Quality of Life : Hedonic Well-Being, Life Satisfaction, and Eudaimonia*. Springer.

Sirgy, M. Joseph, P. Stephanes Kruger, Dong-Jin Lee, and Grace B. Yu. 2011. "How Does a Travel Trip Affect Tourists' Life Satisfaction?" *Journal of Travel Research* 50 (3). SAGE Publications Ltd: 261–75.

Society, Royal. 2012. "People and the Planet."

Sprott, David, Sandor Czellar, and Eric Spangenberg. 2009. "The Importance of a General Measure of Brand Engagement on Market Behavior: Development and Validation of a Scale." *Journal of Marketing Research*. Vol. XLVI.

Taylor, Charles. 2007. *A Secular Age*. Cambridge Univ Press.

Twenge, Jean M., W Keith Campbell, and Elise C Freeman. 2012. "Generational Differences in Young Adults' Life Goals, Concern for Others, and Civic Orientation, 1966-2009." *Journal of Personality and Social Psychology* 102 (5): 1045–62.

White, Nicholas. 1995. "Conflicting Parts of Happiness in Aristotle's Ethics." *Ethics*.

Wilczek, Frank. 2016. *A Beautiful Question : Finding Nature's Deep Design*.

Witt, Ulrich. 2010. "Symbolic Consumption and the Social Construction of Product Characteristics." *Structural Change and Economic Dynamics* 21 (1): 17–25.

CPSIA information can be obtained
at www.ICGtesting.com
Printed in the USA
JSHW041214201120
9680JS00005B/36